On the Brink

Andy Sibbald

Published in Canada by Lunatic Publishing
Copyright @ 2020 by Andy Sibbald
All rights reserved including the right to reproduce
this book or portions thereof in any form whatsoever.

Please address queries to:
Lunatic Publishing
#105, 1130 Pandora Avenue
Victoria, BC Canada
V8V 3R1

Cover design by Iryna Spica
Typeset at SpicaBookDesign

ISBN 9798688846034

Printed and bound with KDP

My Thanks To

*Iryna Spica for the cover art and her layout
and design work*

*Dave Henry and Simon Shepherd for
proofreading this book.*

Other Books by Andy Sibbald

For Teens

Ishigaq: The Quest for Home
Ishigaq: Nipster's Magical Cane
Ishigaq: Following Nipster's Dream

For Adults

Grease My Hooves: Politics in Canada
Wen Shen: The Queen of Wu Kang
One Soldier's Journey: The Canadian Forestry Corps
The Catholic Abuse of Filipino Women
Prejudice, Racism, Exclusion and Exploitation
The Quest for Social Responsibility

The 'Every Village Needs and Idiot' Collection
Ms. Stinky Does Esquimalt
The Quack of Quadra Village
Uncle Ponzi: The Oaf of Oak Bay
The Quack of Quadra Village
The Langford Lush
"Foxy" Visits Mongolia
The Jackass of James Bay
The Dockside Green Dummy
Luna Tick: The Witch of Vic West
Ms. Stinky Goes to the Slammer
The Fernwood Fanatic
The Greater Esquimalt Drunken Seagulls
Tofino to Tokyo
The Quack of Quadra Village

The 101 Series
Self-Serving Religion 101
Dirty Contracting 101

Introduction

If you are like me, you have noticed that not only the world and technology we are using are rapidly changing, but so too is the environment we live in in North America. I am not referring to the changes we see in the physical environment, but rather an increasing dissatisfaction with the political and economic status quo. At present these problems seem to be much more severe in the United States and the response to them is unprecedented. Like lava gurgling under the surface of the earth, ready to erupt, political, economic and social problems have now risen to a point where there will be a massive societal eruption if many things do not change.

There have been many comparatively minor incidents, but also some major expressions of dissatisfaction with the way politicians and those who control the economy are carrying out their business. We see young people choosing not to have kids because they do not want them to experience the future. Global warming is apparently responsible for major negative changes in the weather but the political will seems to be lacking to do much about it. Middle class jobs are disappearing and many have no chance of buying homes or gaining anything more than a minimum-wage paying job. This is a particularly bitter pill to swallow if they have basically borrowed the equivalent of half a mortgage to pay for their education so that they can spend the next ten years working in the corner store down the street for minimum wage and no benefits or pension plan.

Things have changed and there is growing discontent internationally. Society has gone through phases in my life where people, couples and countries have tried to work things out and fix them. Then we moved into the phase where everything, including relationships, is disposable and things are discarded before things can be worked out and fixed. Ask your grandchild what a cobbler is! Now we seem to be into a phase where major confrontation appears to be where we are headed. Like a bad marriage, things have reached a point where enough is enough for many individuals, groups and countries. There is a lower degree of tolerance for where we find ourselves socially and economically, and for those with whom we share massive philosophical differences about where we should be headed as individuals, groups and countries.

In North America we do not have national leaders who are capable of being creative to the degree they need to be, to find solutions to our pressing problems. We need a major paradigm shift and there will be major resistance from those who feel that the present system is working just fine. The question is, for whom is it working just fine? It is time we are honest about the shelf life of our economic system, needing a complete political overhaul, developing a more inclusive political system where power is more broadly shared and it is the citizenry that calls the shots. There needs to be international cooperation when tackling big issues like famine, global warming and collectively dealing with countries that sell arms to other countries that create refugees and massive poverty. It is a time for honesty, accountability, creativity and massive change!

Table of Contents

The Escalation

There is a huge array of political and economic systems across the world. From monarchies and democracies to totalitarian regimes and dictatorships. There are economic systems ranging from basic barter systems to highly complex ones based on supply and demand with monetary economies, stock markets and fluctuating commodity prices. Since politics began there have been different ideas about the best way to govern people and how economies involving groups of people should be operated. These systems were likely forced to evolve as specialization, population increases and greater mobility occurred. There are often very different ideas about which are the most effective political systems and how economies are best managed.

So politics and economics have always been areas of debate and conflict.

There have been similar debates in other areas, and to a large degree they have determined the ways in which societies have evolved. A very basic example is if we believe man is basically bad and will do the wrong thing left to his own devices, the approach we take to developing communities and their institutions will be very different than if we believe man is inherently good and prone to doing the right thing. Our thoughts about these types of things shape our values and the types of political systems and institutions created. Almost all economic systems are based on supply and demand. The problem is that some of these market economies are based on the idea that consumption must continue ever escalating. Generally speaking, the greater the amount of supply beyond what is immediately required, the lower the price of a commodity or service. When there is a demand that exceeds the supply of a commodity or service, the greater the price. A market economy creates competition and economic wars and scenarios that may be good for business but are not necessarily good for communities.

For example, we are seeing right now what happens to oil prices if there is a glut of oil on the market. The price drops. Through this process damage can be done to the economies of other countries. For example, if Russia and the Organization of the Oil Exporting Countries decide they want to hurt the economy of Canada and the United States they can flood the market with oil which will severely diminish the revenues of many oil-producing nations. If Canada and the United States decide to pump more oil to make up for their revenue shortfalls caused by the glut of oil already on the market, they risk further lowering the price if they increase the supply of oil even further.

Other systems are about subsistence and are only concerned about economic growth to the point where needs can be met. In traditional cultures production may be linked to population growth and particularly where there is not a monetary economy. Profit may be an odd concept to aboriginal peoples still living traditional lives in the Amazon and elsewhere. Some people are content when they have their basic needs met.

There are also cases where communities are not served well by market economies. I recall the excitement in a community where a mine that had been closed had been purchased by a large multi-national mining company. Many miners and their families who had left the community after the mine had closed envisioned going back to work, families moving back to the community and local businesses thriving again. Sadly, none of this materialised because there was an abundance of lead and zinc on the market at the time, and so to have reopened this mine would have resulted in further lowering the price of both metals. Since the company that bought the mine owned other lead zinc mines it felt its shareholders would be best served by mothballing the mine for good. In a global economy you can see businesses closed overnight if they cannot compete with new suppliers in countries where labour costs are much lower.

With globalization, workers in one part of the world can be impacted by supply chains in other parts of the world they may not even be aware of. For example, there may be metal components for a specific brand of watch originating from one mine in one country. If there is a strike at the mine, or a ship sinks that is carrying the watch components, this may put the production of these watches on hold on an entirely different continent. This could result in lay-offs that watch factory workers cannot understand because all seemed well at the plant where they work. As globalisation has increased, workers are more removed from the means of production and market forces that often control their fate, and there is little they can do about it. There are success stories like the Harmac pulp mill in Nanaimo, British Columbia, Canada that was purchased by the employees and then successfully operated by the employees when the owner of the company planned to close it. These types of success stories are quite rare because the factors that often result in business closures often can not be addressed locally because they are occurring in other countries. For example, a new factory is opened in Japan and it is state of the art and highly efficient, with a need for about 50% less workers than an old factory in Canada that has out-dated equipment, higher wages and declining production.

The question is whether a global economy is better than many national economies. There are many answers to this question and it depends on who you ask. For example, if you ask a consumer, they may be happy with the inexpensive products from China found in many North American stores. Workers in North America, who produce similar items and are at threat of losing their jobs due to this competition, may not be in favour of a global economy. Shareholders of companies that produce goods likely support globalisation because the cheaper the components are for their products, the more money they should presumably make.

In terms of economics on a personal level, there have also been major changes. There is tremendous personal debt and money is being hoarded to generate more money. Money is not necessarily being rein-vested in the economy to buy products and services, to build and to repair, the way it used to be, thereby creating needed community resources, local jobs and prospering businesses. Money is being taken from the economy and invested, stashed in offshore accounts that deny the country where the income was generated tax dollars, and being used to make more money in the Third World, where there is horrific exploitation, like dangerous mines, massive deforestation, palm oil plantations and massive damage to aboriginal people and the environment through the pursuit of fossil fuels.

The boss may live down the street in Toronto, but if you are working for a multi-national company they may be in New York, Beijing or London. The local sawmill may have gone from local ownership to being owned nationally, along with other mills, to being owned by a multi-national company. This change, for what was a local business, means that it is now subject to forces and international complexities understood by few who actually work there, leading to a sense of helplessness and uncertainty.

We have seen single crop starvation when family garden plots were replaced by single commod-ity growth, like coffee, that could not be eaten when the price of coffee plummeted or crops were wiped out by bad weather. Not only that but planting the same crop, time and time again results in the depletion of some nutrients in the soil, necessitating the need for chemical fertilizers and all the problems that they cause in local bodies of water with fish stocks and other marine life.

Most political and economic systems have their pros and cons, although there are some political systems where it is difficult to find any pros. Systems that began in one way have evolved into systems that are becoming less useful as time progresses. These are the basis for some of the present discontent and speak to the need for massive changes.

Unhealthy Approaches

Governments generally do not like demonstrations in response to their actions for obvious reasons. This is true of both democratic and communist governments, although communist responses have often been harsher. In democracies, people are technically free to express their discontent although there have been increasing attempts over the years to reduce this right, and democratic rights, generally. This has been done through legislation but has also been done through underhanded approaches. One such approach is to use plants at protests to discredit them and the organizations holding them. The actions of violent demonstrators can deliberately turn what would have been a peaceful demonstration into one that the media characterizes as violent. This type of thing happens a lot more than you might think. For example, if one political party wants to discredit another, it may have some agitators show up at their national convention and cause problems. In other cases, plants are used to discredit an organization by confronting the police watching over the demonstration, or by looting and breaking store windows right in front of reporters. The plants will often wear facemasks and this too can detract from an organization's credibility and claims that a group had intended to hold a peaceful demonstration. Since this has happened a number of times, many people will recognize that people who are wearing facemasks in demonstrations and who misbehave are seldom part of the organization that organized it. It is also important to remember that while an incident within a protest, intended to discredit an organization may only take a minute, there may only be a fifteen second segment on television to cover the incident. When people see the fifteen-second segment it suggests that the small isolated incident was but a small example of how the protest got out of hand.

A filmmaker recorded a demonstration in Quebec. After the demonstration was over all kinds of negative claims were made about the group that held the demonstration because it had turned violent. The group that held the demonstration claimed that the people who had caused trouble at the demonstration were not from the group. This claim was not initially taken seriously, but then the man who filmed the demonstration caught on film that the two instigators of the problems were wearing police boots and had nothing to do with the group. This is an example of how one group can try to damage the credibility of another. There are many other dirty tricks that can be used by groups that oppose other groups. Having people on social media that discredit organizations and their ideas is but one example. When I travelled in Asia I often saw signs offering employment to hackers.

There is also what I like to think of as the passive aggressive approach and the aggressive approach. President Trump has provided good examples of both. When people waving flags and banners that were consistent with supporting the Republican Party protested at the Michigan Legislature, toting guns, Trump said he shared their belief that people needed to get back to work and failed to comment on them bringing guns to the rally. So he aggressively supported the rally but ignored the fact that guns were being wielded publicly. He also failed to acknowledge that the people with guns, who for the most part support him, were acting as a serious threat to public safety. It is like when horrible racist comments are made, or numerous people are gunned down and he says nothing, when a leader would have condemned these acts.

I will never forget when 9-11 occurred. The President's response was something to the effect that war had been declared on the United States. This was inaccurate but the response to 9-11 has resulted in all kinds of legislation being introduced in response to terrorism that often also has the power to curtail our rights, invade our privacy and deny us due process. I strongly believe it is a mistake to bring in legislation that is not specific enough to both deal with terrorism but also protect human rights. For example, The Patriot Act allows the United States to confiscate computers, cell phones and hold people without due process as long as it is deemed necessary. Deemed necessary by who and for how long? While this could be helpful to deal with terrorists, what if someone like Trump decides that anyone who did not vote for the Republicans is a terrorist? If I am travelling to the United States, what are the grounds for taking my computer and cell phone at the border? Many people might suggest I am being paranoid and have nothing to worry about, but there are many people with many different problems who thought something would never happen to them. As long as the law says these things are possible, and I do not clearly know the criteria through which they are applied, I must assume they could be applied to me. Much has to do with how the terms in the law are defined and how they are interpreted. Who and what is a terrorist is a critical question with the present United States Government. Who and what is a threat to national security? I have been told that all kinds of legislation are being put through while we are distracted by COVID-19. This has been a Trump approach since he got in. He creates smokescreens and while attention is diverted, pushes through self-serving, or harmful legislation. So it is easy to see how some people would be fearful of major events like COVID-19 and protests against the police, because they are accustomed to major events being used as a justification for diminishing the rights of the citizenry, or quietly pushing through legislation legislators do not want the citizenry to know about.

For example, there is talk about having cell phone apps that will track whether someone has been in contact with someone with COVID-19. There may also be the potential to see whether or not people are adhering to social distancing guidelines where it is the law. It is easy to see how contact tracing would be helpful via a smartphone but the potential abuses of this app could be huge. Everything from stalking to the elimination of privacy as we know it could occur with this type of application. I could see advertisers wanting access to see what stores shoppers frequent so they can personalize ads accordingly. People in demonstrations and meetings could be monitored. It is scary and I hope this app will not be used, but if it is brought in, it will be done under the guise of protecting us and keeping us safe, when what it does do is create the ultimate "Big Brother is Watching You" scenario. Given the apparent desire by some to turn the United States into a police state, this is even more frightening.

If you think about the scenarios I have mentioned, it is not as though the people and their governments are on the same page, or that they share the same goals within a democratic framework. It is as though the electorate are having things done to them that are often not in their best interests. I believe this is being done out of fear in the case of the application I referred to. Politicians should be fearful that at some point people will have had enough of a small minority of very wealthy people enjoying tax breaks provided by their cronies while more people go hungry, end up homeless and with no hope. All the laws and measures to control terrorism and "keep people safe" can as easily be applied within a country's borders and used to oppress and beat down opposition. So, when things get ugly, as they inevitably will, with an unsustainable economy that is eliminating the middle class, the rich want to have laws that can be used to control the people who are not happy about the rich become richer and the pool of poor multiplying many times over every year. Creating new laws that can be used to oppress opposition internally is not the answer. The answer is to look at the economy and ask how it can be changed, or replaced to one that is sustainable and does not create billionaires and others with nowhere to live and no food. It is time to redefine what economic growth means and not take convenient statistics to point how well we are doing without also looking at the grim reality in inner cities and impoverished areas. The wealth being generated obviously is not helping everyone and that is not acceptable. We have an economy that requires a cheap pool of labour and there is always going to be a group of unemployed workers and poor to fill this need. This is a problem because the economy is built on some not having jobs and the means to provide for their basic needs. Nowadays some people have three jobs and they still cannot pay the rent and feed their families.

I recall reading about a black mother in the United States who lived in the "projects" in some American city. She had a young boy who she wanted to have opportunities that she had never had, and in order to do that was working three minimum wage jobs, and her son would go home and take the key from under the rug to let himself in. One day the young boy was attacked and the mother was raked over the coals for leaving him alone. She would not have had to, had one job been enough for her to pay the rent and put food on the table but this was not the case. I recall thinking how sad the situation was. If the mother had stayed home and gone on welfare that would have been wrong but if she gained enough work to meet their basic needs with a bit extra for her son's benefit that was wrong because it required leaving him unsupervised. With a little help and a living minimum wage, the mother, who obviously had a great work ethic, could have worked, looked after her son and saved a little for his education.

This situation when compared to the tax breaks giving to the wealthy is one of the reasons there is simmering dissent that is going to bubble to the surface if things do not change.

Occupy Canada was an example of what I am talking about. However, the movement lacked leadership and became scattered as people wanted to include far too many issues under the same umbrella. With solid leadership and an unwavering focus on political and economic issues a movement like that could have achieved a lot more. It will take time to develop the cohesion and focus necessary for groups like this to become far more effective, because instigating social change often requires trial and error. There are many lessons to be learned from Occupy Canada's attempt at instigating social change. Eventually, after enough attempts, a very intelligent, cohesive plan will emerge to address the economic and political problems as seen through the eyes of an increasing number of disenfranchised citizens. It is not if this will happen, but rather when this will happen.

Ignorance and Anger

As I watch the United States, I wonder to what degree Russia is involved beyond the election interference. When the President goes out of his way time and time again to divide the country in numerous different ways, to create a massive debt and to verbally abuse China, allies and many international organizations, he serves as a huge embarrassment to many United States citizens. They rightly expect the President to set an example and to be an international leader. Many of Trump's actions and those of his administration must make Putin quite happy. It is as though everything that can be done to undermine democracy in the United States is being done. If actions are taken that do not benefit the United States, or in fact hurt the country, it is logical to ask why the actions were taken and who is benefiting, if the United States citizenry is not. The lies and lack of credibility of some in the White House make it clear that international credibility is not high on the list of priorities.

Claims that there was proof that the COVID-19 virus originated in a lab in Wuhan, China, by the President and Secretary of State, proved to be totally untrue, and the so-called proof the Secretary of State claimed existed was never produced. This attack on China is being used as a distraction leading up to the 2020 United States election. However, with the trade war worse than ever, and the relationship with China already terrible, blaming China for a large number of virus-related problems to hide Trump's incompetence is clearly not the answer. If he continues doing this for personal gain and to distract voters from the terrible economic situation in the United States, there may come a point where all Americans pay for this if China decides to retaliate. It sounds like the virus was transferred from an animal in a wet market to a human being and then spread in Wuhan. If this is the case, what should be of the most concern internationally is that China takes measures to ensure this does not happen again. I am tired of listening to Trump blame China, Obama and anyone else that serves as a distraction from his bungling of the COVID-19 situation, the tanking economy, unresolved trade issues and social, health and educational program cuts, racial inequality and his blatant incompetence.

Trump fires people when they are looking into things that create discomfort by ensuring he is accountable, and verbally abuses people in his own party if they disagree with him. Obviously, this is seen as acceptable conduct by many, but I see a once proud nation headed for bankruptcy and, a greatly diminished international role. It is not even clear to me who the United States considers its allies to be, and if they have maintained the ones they had before Trump. If so, it is only because diplomats and others have worked behind the scenes around him. He has told many world leaders how to do their jobs, which is ironic when he clearly has no idea how to do his own. He is an insecure petty man who is self-centred in the extreme and suffers from delusions of grandeur.

Having said all that, it would logically follow that President Trump will be ousted in the 2020 election and that the United States will return to a more civil society. Unfortunately, logic has nothing to do with it. Many Trump supporters and others only realize they have been lied to and deceived when they are impacted on a personal level. Like the man who apparently took chemicals in Arizona based on the President's promotion of them for COVID-19 and then died. I doubt his wife, who took the same chemicals and apparently ended up in intensive care but lived, will be voting Republican in 2020. There is a difference between lies and misinformation but the end result can be painfully the same.

Since President Trump was elected there has been an on-going attack on the educational system in the United States. I cannot recall seeing one article involving the United States Secretary of Education where she has done something that helps to improve the public education system, made managing student loans easier during COVID-19, or advocated for more educational funding for public schools. The articles I have read have mentioned what I perceive attacks on the public education system and the support for private schools, and what are little more than diploma mills. She is very big on private schools, but then, she is rich. These are obviously not accessible to most citizens. I perceived her actions as part of a broader Republican agenda that is starting to pay off for some within the Party. That strategy is dumbing down the population and watering down public education and supporting non-accredited universities. So the wealthy, predominantly white kids will still have their private schools and everyone else will have an increasingly poor public educational system due to neglect and massive cuts. It is like everything else with this administration because many are very wealthy. They want a system for the rich and generous funding for it, generated by taking money from public programs and services that benefit all. It is a disgrace and is part of the reason that dissention will rise to dangerous levels in the future.

Dumbing down the population will result in a greater number of Trump supporters. So, the ideal person from a Republican political perspective is likely uneducated, angry, believes they are being persecuted and simply needs to be told a conspiracy theory that plays into what they already believe. The end result is wanting to see "the swamp drained". Apparently, this includes ensuring brain drain continues at a rapid pace in the administration via firings and refilling the swamp via nepotism and often with people with shady pasts and scant qualifications. So the "swamp has been drained" and "America has been made great again" with huge COVID-19 numbers compared to any other country and the economy in very serious trouble. Agencies and Departments are expected to support the position of the President even when they are supposed to be non-partisan or who have experts whose opinions differ from those of the President. For example, the Attorney General has been challenged by many in the legal profession for what they consider to be a lack of neutrality. This will play out over time and it will be interesting to see what, if any, consequences there will be for William Barr. Of course, the previous Attorney General, Jeff Sessions, fell out of favour with the President when he recused himself from the Russia probe. While I do not like Jeff Sessions due to his involvement in the Deferred Action for Childhood Arrivals (DACA), program, recusing himself was the right thing to do. Another example involves the clash between the President and the White House administration with the Centre for Disease Control (CDC), where scientists created a report that outlined the steps needed to open businesses and all types of other agencies and facilities with COVID-19 still being a major problem. This report apparently did not support the quick reopening of the economy that the President had in mind, and as a result the CDC report was actually released the day the 50th state began reopening. Politics overrode science and medicine, and the report was received far too late by the states to be of much use. Scientists have warned about a second wave of the virus if businesses are reopened too quickly. Fortunately, Governors call the shots that determine the speed with which reopening's occur, contrary to a claim the President made that he does.

Ignorance and anger are running wild in the United States. You have gun toting Trump supporters showing up at the Michigan Legislature demanding that businesses be reopened, while many do not practice social distancing. I saw one of the demonstrators interviewed who thought that COVID-19 was a Democratic Hoax intended to hurt Trump's chances of re-election. A seed that was likely planted by one television station that is pro Republican to a point of stupidity, and comments shared on social media. The demonstration was sad, with the people waving Trump and Confederate flags, presumably not realizing that many may lose their health care and food stamps while at the same time the Republican Party has given a massive tax break to the wealthy. Angry but unfortunately ignorant people. The saying, rebel without a cause comes to mind. All these people needed was someone like Trump to come along, spread conspiracy theories and give them a common cause to galvanize around and focus them. That, and the sense that they finally have a leader they can relate too even though he is a billionaire and they are desperate to get back to work. It is ironic that people like this should have any use for Trump given that it is people like him that are often blamed for the lot of the poor.

Unfortunately, the peaceful people who went to the Michigan Legislature without guns because they wanted the economy to reopen, and were fearful of having no income were lost in the broader scene. It reminded me of Occupy Canada, to the extent that there were peaceful people whose message was lost due the extreme behaviour of others who joined the group but in doing so discredited it. This resulted in the peaceful people in Michigan wasting their time because their message was not newsworthy by comparison to people toting guns and making threats. Since there was seemingly no police or military response to this armed demonstration, I expect there will be more of the same thing, and find myself asking if this is what the majority of Americans want. I certainly doubt it. In spite of the people in the United States being adamant about their gun rights, the vast majority are peace-loving people like you find anywhere else. Attacks by the President on the Democratic Governor in Michigan clarified for me why the President had supposedly supported the protesters desire to get back to work in their MAGA hats and waving their Confederate flags.

People wonder why Trump's base supports him in spite of on-going abuses and corruption but there really is a simple formula. The formula requires a certain type of individual to join Trump's base. Put simply these people must see themselves as victims of the government. They identify Trump as the man that can, and will, address all their concerns and in doing so stop their on-going persecution so that they too may enjoy all the benefits that they have been denied but so richly deserve in their minds. I suspect they do not watch CNN, or read major national newspapers in the United States because if they did, they would see they are being hurt for the benefit of the wealthy. No need to cloud the issue with facts and Fox News tells them all they need to know. Facts will not stop the momentum of Trump's base at this point because many have needs that are being met by being part of his base. Many of Trump's supporters are not the type of people one would think of as being politically astute so why are they involved in politics to an extent they likely never have been before?

It is a simple formula-shared ignorance, a shared desire for increased power, shared anger, shared conspiracy theories and a sense of mutual persecution and victimization. This is combined with a desire to live vicariously through Trump who will "Make America Great Again" and "Drain the Swamp." They see Trump like a messiah. Someone who will do for his base what it cannot do for itself because the people in his base enjoy little political power and feel powerless. This is the reason that living vicariously through Trump has such great appeal-a billionaire on your side! Power is provided in two ways to the base. They are given license to spread hate and act in ways that would have been condemned by previous Presidents, via Trump's failures to respond to hateful and often racist behaviour that garners national attention. They also gain power in numbers as they join Trump's base where they meet like-minded people. Perhaps for them it is like when I joined an addictions self-help group and finally met a room full of people that understood "the problem." I felt a sense of belonging and fellowship and perhaps this is what the people in Trump's base feel. Before they were an unorganized group with members scattered randomly across the country with no common cause and now, they are galvanized and have a cause. I think one of the reasons Trump's base will support him regardless of his poor behaviour and incompetence has nothing to do with Trump, but rather has to do with people having their affiliation needs met. Whether they attend a Trump rally, or any other sort of group event they are having their social needs met and feel that very enticing feeling of belonging. They are part of something much bigger themselves that validates their views, seemingly no matter how extreme or divisive.

I think that the toting of guns by Trump supporters was a good illustration of how his base's anger and associated actions should be closely monitored by those responsible for internal terrorism.

Guns and the Government

B eing Canadian, I once applied for and was given a gun license by the government. I got the license because I was living in the Arctic and was trying to support my Inuit wife and our kids the best way I knew how. It was important for us to have fresh wild meat so I started hunting caribou. I did not hunt prior to living in Nunavut and did not hunt after leaving it. I had guns that's specific purpose was hunting and would have never considered buying an assault rifle even if I could have. I was hunting caribou, not people.

I could never understand the United States obsession with guns, even though I am aware of the Second Amendment. I suppose I had never worried about owning a gun because no other law-abiding citizens owned them for things other than hunting, varmint control on farms and for a few other very specific purposes. Every country has illegal guns and it seems they are often owned by gangs who generally shoot each other. So, I did not need a gun to feel safe and never perceived owning one as a right. I was pleased when I received my hunting license because it felt good to know that the government saw me as a solid enough citizen to grant me this privilege.

I was down in Colorado and ran into a man working in a park. He said he was married; had four kids and we discussed many other things. I liked him a lot. He was intelligent, sensible and interesting. I mentioned that I had never understood the U.S. approach to gun ownership, the Second Amendment aside. He was adamant that Americans not only had the right to own guns but needed to own guns. I was thinking to myself-why did I say that and open up that can of worms! Then the man became less animated and essentially said that the United States Government has the military, who are all armed, and if the government does things to United States citizenry that are harmful, the only way they can protect themselves is by owning guns. He pointed out that the Nazis had confiscated the guns of people in countries they had occupied during the Second World War so that they had no means of defending themselves, or organizing an armed resistance. I can understand his point because we do see governments turn on their own people and if they are not armed, they have no way of defending themselves. On the other hand, this is a far cry from the mass shootings occurring in schools, places of worship and elsewhere. His point did not include the National Rifle Association trying to defend the mass ownership of guns, regardless of how much gun violence there is in the United States. I am sure he would have acknowledged that some people with severe mental health problems should not own guns but at the same time it is not uncommon to see militia groups in the United States on television armed to the teeth. It is also not uncommon to hear all the politicians talking about sending prayers to the victim's families of gun violence with no intention of supporting any legislation that would decrease it.

The people in the United States who showed up armed to a demonstration in front of the Michigan State Legislature did not need to protect themselves from the government. The government had not shown up with guns and challenged the demonstrators right to be there to voice their dissent and exercise their First Amendment rights. Perhaps this is what we can expect in the future but in much larger numbers. So, while I understand the Colorado man's position, and it makes sense to me, the mass killings and wielding of guns at public events is something completely different. Having guns to defend oneself from anyone, or any entity is passive, whereas mass shootings and the wielding of guns publicly with no imminent threat is not.

I do not profess to be an expert on the United States or its gun control laws but it seems there are two major problems. The first is that with rights must come responsibilities, and the second is United States politicians who are only too happy to take election donations from the National Rifle Association. It may appear that I am off on a tangent but we are talking about dissent increasing in North America. It is one thing to have dissent expressed through peaceful demonstrations but quite another to have it expressed by gun wielding fanatics. It will not be people like the man I met from Colorado who will be the problem because he is a stable, rational person. It is much more likely to be Trump's base, which takes in a wide swath of right-wing ideology from the mild to the extreme. Dissent without mass gun ownership has far fewer potential consequences.

I was surprised at what appeared to be very little response to people carrying guns at the Michigan Legislature, and the fact that they were allowed to do so when the Democratic Michigan Governor had been threatened a number of times prior to this. It seemed unruly and so out of control. It made no sense to me that so few can put so many in dangers in a democratic society. It was all about the individual right of gun ownership undermining the collective right to safety and freedom from armed intimidation. It is the love of guns and few restrictions in many places in the United States on the types of guns owned which is one of the reasons why I believe there may very well be a civil war in the United States, or an armed standoff if Trump loses the 2020 election. Trump has engaged in aggressive, intimidating behaviour, and encouraged other to do so, via failing to respond to it negatively as a good leader would do, or adding fuel to the fires on Twitter. Meanwhile his wife is running her anti-bullying nonsense when the biggest bully in the United States is her husband.

Aggression breeds aggression and the United States is a powder keg that has become increasingly volatile over the past few years. I suspect that countries like China and Russia have realized that all they need to do is wait for the United States to implode and no action is required on their part. The United States will do to itself what China or Russia could not do without starting a world war. China has always been long on patience and with a communist government can play this game far longer than a President with a four-year term likely on his way out due to his incompetence and destruction of the United States both internally and globally. China's success dealing with COVID-19 was in large part because, unlike the United States, collective rights supersede individual rights and so dealing with the virus was about the health of all and it was understood that many individuals would be inconvenienced for the benefit of all. In the United States there have been demonstrations about the loss of individual rights as governments try to deal with COVID-19. Some politicians have opened the economy and churches far to soon due to pressure around individual rights, and in an attempt to maintain support from the electorate and society as a whole will pay for it. It is a selfish approach but then when you look at the President, there is no one who is more concerned about himself and who puts his wants and needs before those of the collective more frequently.

When you have large groups, including countries, that put the needs and rights of individuals before collective rights there is eventually bound to be conflict. This is because at some point your selfishness will interfere with mine, and I will conclude that you are an impediment that needs to be removed. This mentality moves the United States closer to the brink.

The Old Boys' Network

I have often wondered how I would feel if I were a woman listening to old white-haired male politicians discussing women's reproductive health and feeling that it is remotely appropriate that they should do so without any women present. I am tired of people like Moscow Mitch McConnell and other United States Senators taking measures to hurt others and doing nothing to support bills that would make the lives of average Americans better. Moscow Mitch and Trump will die soon and they are leaving a terrible mess for young people to clean up. Having pulled out of arms control deals, environmental accords intended to curtail global warming, and promoting the use of oil and coal, while stripping the country of many environmental protections that do things like protecting clean drinking water, there is catastrophe waiting to happen. It is the "me" mentality of politicians that is killing the country because there is little consideration for future generations, or even the health and welfare of citizens today. The attacks on Obamacare have left millions without health care and where is the better health care plan Trump bragged about? There is nothing to replace Obamacare while COVID-19 is ravaging the country but I suspect that the Republicans could care less. Trump has always been jealous of Obama and whether this is because he is racist, or because he is incompetent and lacks intelligence by comparison is puzzling. He does feel that the same criticisms he made of Obama, about things like his days golfing, should not be applied to him. Whether this is because he thinks he is better than Obama, because Obama is black, or because he thinks he should not be subject to the same standards, he expects of others is unclear.

What is clear is that racism is coming out of the closet as COVID-19 spreads across the United States and Canada. There have been racist attacks on Chinese citizens in both countries. The difference is that the Prime Minister of Canada and the Premier of British Columbia have condemned this racism and have both said that it has no place in Canada. It most certainly doesn't! I was glad they addressed this issue. I cannot recall Trump condemning any racist activities in the United States. His silence makes him complicit when there are horrible incidents involving white nationalism and other activities that are pro-white, anti-everyone else and he says nothing. His position makes it incumbent on him to condemn racism for the betterment of the country and the safety of the citizenry but he often won't. Even if he condemns racism at this point it is too late and people will assume, he is only doing so to garner votes, and they will be right. I would put it in the same league with him being a "Christian", when I observe his on-going behaviour!

I recall a General in the United States Army stating that he essentially did not care what he was ordered to do if it was illegal because he would refuse. This was encouraging because while the armed forces take orders from the United States government it is good to know that illegal activities will not be supported and that the armed forces may actually be a force for logic and reason should a civil war start. So far, the Democrats have filed some lawsuits, impeached Trump and have done a few other things but he has been getting away with all kinds of abuses. There will come a point when this will go to far and there will be serious backlash from across the country. For example, all that needed to happen at the Michigan Legislature was for a bunch of anti-Trump demonstrators to show up armed to confront the pro-Trump supporters and there likely would have been killings. The left has really been doing very little that curtails the aggression of the right but there will come a time when they have had enough of the stupidity and aggression, and may very well retaliate.

Moscow Mitch McConnel was heckled in a Kentucky restaurant while having supper with his wife and the co-owner of the Red Hen restaurant in Lexington, Virginia, asked former White House Press Secretary Sarah Sanders to leave the restaurant. This would have likely never happened ten years ago but is an example of the degree to which people are tired of political corruption, lying, and the on-going sense of entitlement among some in politics. It also speaks to the serious divisions in the country and the degree of healing that will be required to create any sort of national cohesion. The level of frustration has escalated, and I have read many reports that talk about politicians, and even people like Dr. Fauci, Director of the National Institute of Allergy and Infectious Diseases, needing increased security. Could this be because people do not think the government has any interest in listening to them, or acting on their concerns? Has it come to a point where people level threats, rather than write letters because they feel so removed from the democratic process that they must threaten extreme action to be heard? Obviously, something is radically wrong but when people hear the

President name calling and denigrating others it is likely that others feel they have been given license to treat people disrespectfully and threaten them due to the example being set at the top.

When I refer to the United States as a powder keg, I am not referring to one large group getting upset and lashing out. I am talking about a groundswell of dissent amongst huge numbers of people in many walks of life. There are many groups that are angry for a variety of reasons and they are being pushed to the brink. People can only be pushed so far and at some point will have had enough. There may also be many alliances formed between groups that have been the recipients of the same sort of political abuse. As one massive cohesive group forms people will feel empowered by the numbers of people who share their views. The group will gain more members and more and more momentum. All that will need to happen will be for a horrific event to galvanize many individuals and groups of people who feel they have been abused. In a matter of days things have the potential to get very nasty and of course everyone could access guns and plenty of ammunition. It as though each day simply puts more fuel on the fire as we hear more lies, more inaccuracies about cures for COVID-19, about more black deaths at the hands of police and about more corruption and political abuse. The George Floyd killing has done some of this but I think there will be another incident and that will be the final straw. The George Floyd protests will look mild by comparison and the country will either rethink the whole system or it will implode due to internal violence. The George Floyd demonstrations are serving to show people the power they have and that when united they can force change. So, George Floyd's death will not be in vain because some changes are being made, but more importantly, those involved in the protests can see what is possible with collective action.

It is old politicians running the United States into the ground. Along with legislation to stop lobby groups and corporations from buying politicians, younger politicians with kids who will be around for the next sixty years need to be elected. This will ensure that environmental issues will be given their due, new ideas and energy will abound and the old boys' network will finally be disbanded for good. Stronger rules about nepotism are required and so are those that hold the President accountable. Change can either occur peacefully, or the powder keg will continue gaining pressure. This is what is likely to happen because most politicians, and especially those clearly on the take, will not willingly give up the goodies they are accustomed to receiving for their election campaigns in exchange for votes in support of corporations and lobby groups. If changes are not made peacefully, they will occur after a major conflict. When the US citizenry reviews what went wrong afterwards, what will immediately become apparent are the abuses of the Republican Party in the past three years along with the contempt the party holds for the public and more specifically those who are not white. I must assume this because when racism is promoted at the top the rank and file in the Republican Party remain silent as they always do. It seems that Mitt Romney is the only person in the Republican Party with a backbone and of course, as a result, he has been subject to attacks from Trump.

There has been so much corruption and abuse under this administration people have developed a certain degree of complacency around it. It is like when people see it all the time, they become desensitised to lying, racism, misogyny tantrums and stupidity and no longer give it the weight it deserves. I think when Trump is gone, the Republican Party will be a complete mess because no one other than a few tried to defend Republican values, or the Constitution, for that matter. Even at present, the Republican Party is a shell and stands for whatever Donald Trump thinks and says. After Trump and people like Moscow Mitch leave politics, or die, I hope young people will start a new political party to replace what was once the Republican Party. It would really be nice to see a new party that has a moral and ethical foundation and is democratic in all its values. If something like this was organized by young people with contagious energy, enthusiasm and new ideas it could take the country by storm. Any sort of moral leadership would be welcome after the on-going corruption everyone has grown far too accustomed to. It would be so nice to have young, hopeful people with a vision of the future who balance responsibilities with individual and collective rights. The present system is destroying America at an incredibly fast rate. Dumping the old boys' network, what is the Republican Party in name only, and starting again would be great. It may even save the country.

The diversity within the Democratic Party gives me hope and so do the four young ladies of colour who have brought courage, new energy, ideas and a different perspective into United States politics.

Rodney King, George Floyd and Colin Kaepernick

I watch a lot of National Basketball Association basketball and read the news from a few different sources on a daily basis. So George Floyd's death sadly came as no surprise. I have heard on television and read repeatedly about black men being targeted by the police in the same way the First Nations were targeted by police in Saskatoon by the Saskatoon Police Department. The result of this, among other things, was the senseless on-going deaths caused by racism and incredible disrespect for the lives of fellow human beings. In Saskatoon police from the Saskatoon Police Department would arrest a First Nations man (although as far back as 1976 the police did this to a First Nations woman) for drunkenness or disorderly conduct and take them on a *starlight tour*, which involved dropping them off outside the city to try to survive the extremely harsh winter conditions and somehow make it back to town safely. Not surprisingly, some died from hypothermia and there has not been one conviction of a police officer for specifically doing this, although one police chief admitted that the practice may have been going on for years. This is a terrible stain on Canadian history.

First Nations people in Canada are unfortunately used to poor treatment and racism. It has been going on for years and in spite of Government apologies and reports by outside bodies about the abuse of First Nations, it continues. I can remember living in Alberta and hearing about how some kids had died from gastroenteritis due to playing in raw sewage in a playground, and there continue to be on-going reports of some First Nations not even having clean drinking water. The United States is not alone when it comes to racism and many Canadian aboriginal people and immigrants have been subject to horrible racism. It never ceases to amaze me that there have been close to 1,200 murders of aboriginal women in Canada over a thirty-three-year period.

In the United States one in 1,000 young black men or boys can expect to get killed by the police. This is an appalling statistic. Ironic that middle- and upper-class whites often tell their kids if they are having a problem and feel scared or in danger, they should tell the police if they see them. I suspect many black parents in the United States tell their kids to stay away from the police no matter what type of danger they are in. This presumably also means that many matters are dealt with within the community and that the police are not involved. Who do you turn to if you do not feel you can safely turn to the police?

When we are talking about police abuses it is useful for me to think back to a book I wrote that had a lot to do with in-groups and out-groups. Within groups like the police it is easy to think that the police are individuals but that everyone outside the group is the same. This does not make sense but is how groups can naturally evolve. It is also natural to think when you are part of a group that is disliked by many that it is you and your colleagues against the world. This is where training and professionalism needs to override these misconceptions and there is no excuse for what happened to Rodney King, George Floyd or surely hundreds or thousands of other minority group members who have been killed or abused by the police. If this type of abuse is rampant between the police and young black men, I would not be surprised if there are also elevated statistics of abuse between the police and aboriginal, Latino and Asian populations. This reminds me of a study I once read that pointed out that many middle-class white kids who committed crimes like vandalism were taken home by the police to parents whom they assumed would deal with their kid. There were many more aboriginal children who were put in youth correctional facilities for similar crimes. I don't know if it was assumed by the police that the First Nations parents would not deal with their kids and address their crimes with them, or they were not home when the police tried to bring their kid home, or why this happened. Racism is likely part of it to some degree.

I am writing this the day after the night of fires in Minneapolis and a few days after the KKK endorsed Trump. I was glad to see that Colin Kaepernick's message has been brought up by Lebron James after people like Trump tried to turn his concern about the treatment of black people by the police into nonsense about disrespecting the flag. I feel Colin Kaepernick did the country a service, and some white team "owners" in the National Football League and Trump wanted to twist his message into something it wasn't to discredit him. He never did get another job in the National Football League after taking a knee during the national anthem. Sometimes I watch things like what Colin Kaepernick did and feel like pulling my hair out as the disinformation starts and the bigots come out of the closet to discredit him. He had, and continues to have, an important message about race relations in America, and since the time he took a knee, things have become a whole lot worse. Trump came out and said it was a terrible thing that happened to George Floyd but with his on-going racism I am sure people can see this is about the election. If he were sincere why did he not condemn the KKK endorsement of him a few days earlier?

I think the Rodney King beating and George Floyd's death sadly bring us all closer to the brink of a very nasty armed confrontation in the United States that I believe will surely happen if Trump remains in office. These incidents are like flashpoints and the next one may be the big one where there is violence all over the United States in response to a racially motivated killing or beating. Other groups may join in that have been marginalized, subjected to on-going racism and other forms of persecution. It is a commonly held belief that racism has been given license by the President through his usual silence when a nasty racially motivated incident occurs or things like the KKK endorsement happen. There were people entering Canada from the United States because they feared for their lives. Many were people of colour and Muslims and I do not blame them. I hope they can enjoy peaceful lives here.

Colin Kaepernick was right to do what he did but many did not want to face the fact that far too many young black men live in fear of the police and are being killed by the police in the United States. In the world of National Football League owners, people like Trump and others, it is easier to twist the message than to face and deal with the grim reality. They come from white privilege, while on a daily basis they make money off the backs of young black men playing sports. They would just as soon not have serious discussions about inequality because their white privilege is all about inequality. The young black men are like commodities. They are traded, sold, drafted and cut. Some make good money, while others are maimed for life via severe injuries, including brain injuries. This while the "owners" make money, and it is relatively well known that no helmet modifications will completely stop life changing head injuries. So, ironically, while Colin Kaepernick was employed by the San Francisco 49ers he had an "owner" who could have traded him or sold him to another team. Does this remind you of something that was abolished years ago, aside from the money the players are making nowadays? It does me, and it makes me sad.

I can only hope that George Floyd's death results in massive change. People need to ask themselves questions like why is it okay for white men with assault rifles to hang around the front of the Michigan Legislature when a black man with no gun is being killed by police a short time later in a nearby state?

Black and aboriginal people have been abused for hundreds of years. What surprises me is that there have not been a great many more demonstrations and riots. Perhaps, when people see the abuses first hand via the media they are far more likely to respond angrily and take to the streets. It seems that there are likely a number of factors that must be present for situations like the ones involving Rodney King and George Floyd to escalate out of control, because the killing of young black men by the police happens with far greater frequency than you may think.

The Failed Social Experiment

I often see United States citizens on television claiming that the United States is the greatest country on the planet. Yes, but for who? The black woman in the projects having trouble making ends meet with two minimum wage jobs, the 113,000 homeless people in California or all the minority group members who have been incarcerated even though they are not dangerous offenders? It is a great country if you enjoy white privilege, have health care, have a good job and live in a safe suburb. How many people are actually living the American Dream or the equivalent Canadian Dream?

The United States is a failed social experiment. How could it be anything but this when for over four hundred years minority groups have been on the outside looking in? As a culture they have not enjoyed economic equality, protection by the government, equality in the eyes of the law, equal access to health care and many other programs and services. There are two types of people when it comes to racism: racists and anti-racists and there is no one in between. What this means is that for four hundred years the racists have held the upper hand and many marginalized people and members of minority groups have not been able to gain equality because they have been oppressed. The American Dream and the idea that anyone in the United States can achieve anything they want is absolute nonsense and always has been. It is part of the rhetoric used by those with white privilege to justify their status in relation to those who have had no chance to even gain equality.

It does not take a rocket scientist to figure out that an economy that creates a small minority of billionaires and over 500,000 homeless people on any given night is not working. This does not include all the people working two and three minimum wage jobs who cannot make ends meet, those surviving on food stamps and those who simply cannot do it anymore. Then there are all the political votes against increasing the minimum wage, while at the same time, the very same politicians vote for pay increases for themselves. A living wage would have gone a long way toward making the lives of the marginalized much more bearable but wealthy politicians would rather give the wealthy a tax break than vote in a living wage for the working poor.

It makes me sick watching Moscow Mitch and Trump and all the other smug political million and billionaires take pleasure in destroying health care for many, refusing to increase wages and making life for the marginalized even more unbearable. It should not come as a surprise that people are angry. Today, as riots happen in many United States cities due to the police killing of George Floyd, I sense that there are many more issues being represented. I also see in these riots many people of different ethnicities and many are young, suggesting that the younger generation has had enough and who can blame them? I also feel the riots are a rejection of what the Republicans have stood for since the election of Trump. It has been the privileged white politicians getting wealthier on the backs of the poor.

....

Young people see people like Trump and the Republicans trash environmental controls, pull out of international arms deals, ignore global warming, pull out of WHO, ratchet up aggression toward China and completely screw up the response to COVID-19 and talk about pulling the armed forces out of Germany, which plays into Russia's hands. Then there was all the Trump stupidity about hydroxychloroquine, ingesting disinfectants, using infra-red light to kill the virus, along with claims that COVID-19 would simply go away, that it was a Democratic Party hoax and that China and the World Health Organization are to blame for all the United States problems with regard to the virus. This is deliberate and is all about distracting people from COVID-19, Trump's many failures and the present economic mess. Trump will apparently do and say anything to increase his chances of winning the 2020 election. This includes doing everything he can to avoid dealing with COVID-19 and being held accountable for his terrible failings. The United States is like a rudderless ship and if it were not for some good Governors, Mayors and other government officials, the situation would be a lot worse than it is. This is because there has been no Federal leadership, and those who could have provided some, like Dr. Anthony Fauci, the Director of National Institute of Allergies and Infectious Diseases, were presumably silenced by the White House Administration. This has created a dangerous situation because if there was ever a time when a Federal coordinated approach was required, it is now.

This situation moves the country closer to the brink of a major disaster and I am not talking about a few police cars being burned and the windows being broken on a few businesses. I am talking about a full-scale armed confrontation between the authorities and those who are disgruntled. The problem the authorities may have is that depending on the issues, they may find that many of their colleagues are sympathetic to the causes of the protesters. Perhaps a soldier's mother has toiled for minimum wage for thirty years; perhaps many black police know of black people who have been gunned down and others know of relatives who have always been homeless. There will be a huge base of people comprised of all walks of life who are legitimately angry. The base will include people of all colours, all sexual orientations, both genders, all religions and all social and economic statuses. There is a growing sense of dissatisfaction in the United States and on May 29, 2020, the country has taken another leap forward toward the brink from which there will be no turning back. The amount of damage to the country since Trump got elected is incredible. The country has gone from the most powerful country in the world, respected by many, to a country that is a mess, is not respected internationally and that is perceived as a part of the problem rather than part of the solution. The country will not work with other countries on global initiatives and blames others like the World Health Organization for its failings.

People are scared and feel insecure. They do not know if the government will help them in tough times. Why would they feel secure when, for example, the Trump administration has done everything it can to eliminate Obamacare, with nothing to replace it during the COVID-19 pandemic? This is a cruel attack on many who without Obamacare will not have health care. So why would the populace have confidence in Trump and his administration?

||||||||||||||||||||||||||||||||||||||||||||||

Amid the COVID-19 pandemic and the George Floyd murder there has been a great deal of concern about the future. Governors and mayors have talked about the need to address the economic issues facing the country and the long legacy of racism. Many have pointed out that the things being said now are the same things that were said when Rodney King was beaten, and nothing changed. I think what I find most appalling is that since we know racism is learned, I have heard nothing about addressing this issue through school curriculums, starting in kindergarten and ending with the last grade of high school. I have heard nothing about the need for a different economic system because the present economic system promotes inequality and always has. I have heard little about how the justice system needs reforming and how this should be done and how to make access to quality health care more equitable. I am saddened by this but suspect that in the end this will end up being nothing more than another step toward the brink.

Chats between politicians, minority group members, the police and others are all good, but these will result in cosmetic changes at best. Governments are good at drawing up plans and creating documents but there is a huge need for creativity. If you think about it the police, the government and economies are structured and are governed by huge numbers of rules and laws. Involving only people who work within structured entities to make reforms will make it far less likely that there will be the types of creative solutions required to the present problems.

People who are highly creative and who do not come from highly structured systems are needed. The economy does not need tweaking. What is needed is a new economy created by a new vision that ensures the equitable distribution of income and opportunity. Equitable access to health care will not be addressed through a few policy changes. When you have health care that must be paid for, you get economic segregation and also racial segregation. Minority group members use public health clinics while those with health care and good incomes can access private medical care. Economics play a huge role in the disparity of access to health care. Then you have Trump and Moscow Mitch trying to destroy Obamacare with nothing to replace it. The justice system needs a complete overhaul. Calling it a "justice" system could not be more misleading. The point being that cosmetic changes and banning chokeholds are good, but will the systemic racism across the entire governmental system be addressed? I am sure those who have enjoyed profiting from the present system will be delighted if the reforms are limited to police reforms, but this really misses the entire point, although, as a black lady pointed out to me this morning, the killings of black men is the number one priority and then the other issues can be tackled. I agreed with her but hope that stopping the police from killing black men and boys is just the start or an incredible opportunity will have been missed.

To move forward with an agenda to create real equality in America, the first step must to vote out President Trump and politicians like Moscow Mitch McConnell. The reasons are twofold. Trump has proven to be a racist and it is difficult to imagine him having any sincere interest in making the lives of minority group members better. The second reason is that personal political greed seems to have taken precedence over the needs of the populace generally, so massive tax cuts for the wealthy are perceived as being more important than programs that help and protect the public. A good example is the gutting of the bodies that existed to fight pandemics within the White House.

There needs to be a commitment at all levels of government to address racism, and since it is so wide spread, and since systemic racism is so deeply entrenched it will take time to make meaningful change that will survive in the long term. The same is true of changes to the justice system. Michael Cohen who went to jail for a three-year sentence prior to the pandemic has been released due to the pandemic, but United States jails continue to be filled with members of minority groups, many of whom do not pose any threat to society.

The magnitude of the changes required to stop the momentum toward the brink are absolutely massive. It requires rethinking everything and almost pretending to start the country from square one, but of course history cannot be undone. What can be done is that today, which will soon be history, can be an incremental step in the right direction. The momentum toward the brink must be stopped before intelligent planning can begin; in the same way, intelligent dialogue is not possible while people are still throwing bottles and rocks at the police, looting and vandalizing cities.

Again, the Trump circus must end so that there is national leadership that is committed to working toward racial equality with all levels of government. A national government that leads by example and that puts the welfare of the country before personal gain and partisan politics will go a long way toward making some of the changes possible. I recently wrote a book titled *The Quest for Social Responsibility* and pointed out that the whole United States political system requires changing so that politicians are not bought and paid for by corporations and lobby groups, and will then act on behalf of those who elected them, and not on behalf of those who have greased their palms and paid for their votes. Without fundamental changes to the political system change will not happen. You can see how corrupt the system is when the Republicans oppose mail-in voting in spite of the pandemic, and there are regular attempts by the Republican Party to make it impossible for some citizens of voting age to vote. One of the first things that needs to be decided is whether a truly democratic system will be implemented to replace the appallingly corrupt one in place now. If so, there may be hope. If not, going beyond the brink is simply a matter of time. I have little confidence that the magnitude of changes that are required will be made. There are simply too many people invested in the present system.

I remember as a young person, wondering why many people I talked to all said they supported change, but change never seemed to happen in any major way. The reality often is that the people with the power are benefiting from the status quo and will say they support change but will support minor cosmetic change at best.

Time will tell. If Trump loses the Presidency in 2020 there is still hope. To make the changes necessary will require true love of country, putting self-interest aside and making unpopular decisions that will require tremendous courage. I am hopeful for the future but the work to be done is enormous and will require such creativity and genius it may not be possible.

The Unsociable Social Animals

I f you enjoy nature programs you will have seen many animals ranging from ants to elephants operate collectively for the betterment and safety of the group. You will see bees sting others to protect the hive and die shortly after. You will see wildebeest and zebra mothers re-enter crocodile-infested rivers to look for their offspring. You will see the old matriarch leading a herd of elephants to one of the few drinking holes for miles around. It is pretty easy to predict what would happen if the matriarch decided that it was all about her and charged off with her head full of the information the group needed for survival because she had just decided it was all about her needs and the other herd members didn't matter. She doesn't do this, although among many male animals, including elephants, there are intense competitions for the right to breed. This competition serves to keep the herd strong because only the strongest, healthiest males breed. So many animals cooperate at times but at others compete. The apes are like that also. They compete for breeding rights but often groom each other and travel in troupes. There tend to be pecking orders and we see the same in extended human families. Very few humans are living like wild animals nowadays and there seems to be an abundance of many things, which you would think would negate the need for competition for them. If there are ten apples and five people all would seem to be good, but is it?

All would seem to be good until we apply the economic principles of market forces and supply and demand to the process and remove the people who actually grew the fruit from the sales or bartering process. These few seemingly simple things make the situation so much more complex and I shall use this example to illustrate why there must be a wholesale change to the economic system to address may social ills. In our scenario, the farmers who grow the apples work in an economic system that requires a pool of cheap labour. This pool of cheap labour is beneficial to the farmers who want their apples picked at the lowest possible cost but is harmful to the underemployed and unemployed who comprise the pool of cheap labour. In fact, unemployment has been linked to many health and social problems ranging from insomnia and substance abuse to depression and suicide. Our farmers benefit economically but there is a price to be paid by those who are regularly available for poor paying seasonal work.

Once the ten apples have been picked by the seasonal workers they need to get to market. If there is no marketing board, the laws of supply and demand govern the price of the apples. In this case we have five consumers. If they all want two apples the price will be reasonable but let's say the farmers knew that there were five buyers who each want two apples and they agree to throw out some apples and thereby decrease the supply of apples so that the price goes up. Each consumer still wants two apples but now there are only seven for sale. Conversely, if another farmer came onto the scene and added two apples to the ten there would be twelve apples but only a demand for ten and the price should decrease because the supply exceeds the demand. This basic principle applies to many commodities, like oil, minerals and grain, for example. If there is a glut of a commodity on the market the price decreases, and if there is not enough supply to meet demand the price increases. The ideal is where supply and demand match and good but reasonable prices are paid for products. I will not get into other issues, like all the middlemen wanting to get paid, transportation issues, political espionage through market manipulation, stock exchanges, etc. What is important is that you can see how the economic system can create competition among those producing products and among those consuming them.

We are taught from the time we are children that those who are more successful competing enjoy better lives via the American and Canadian dreams. This is where the justification starts for the inequality we see today because there is a sense that if we win, get the highest grades and excel we are deserving of what we receive. You will notice the individual orientation here. Even if I am part of a team, I am deserving of what I receive as an individual. This can breed a sense of entitlement. It is also erroneous because many of the people I am competing against in school, in athletics, in the workplace and elsewhere have either had a greater or lesser chance to succeed than me due to factors too numerous to mention. We did not start these competitions on a level playing field and as long as we continue to do things this way, we will continue to see major disparities in both opportunities and wealth. If a kid who has had every advantage is competing against some kid from across the tracks, who has one parent in jail and the other on crack, who do you think will win this competition now and for generations to come? The American Dream crap assuages the guilt of those who have all goodies and basically blames those who do not "succeed" no matter how poor their circumstances are growing up. Who believes the lie that we can all be the President or Prime Minister? Not only do the disadvantaged have trouble competing through no fault of their own, but they can also feel guilty about this, thank you to the American Dream.

It is a load of garbage and we need to develop cooperative systems and ways of sharing opportunities through factors other than competition because we will never have a level playing field from which to start a fair competition. This is absolutely essential if we wish to address racial inequality. It is also essential if the trend, whereby the middle class is being eliminated and more and more people are living in abject poverty, is to stop. The same system with the same institutions with the same thinking will always provide the same results. To think otherwise is insanity. So when the rhetoric starts, as it always does, about the need for change after another black man is killed by the police, it will be interesting to see if anyone is willing to tackle those who will try to block real change because it will mean a more equitable distribution of wealth, opportunity, access to health care, equal treatment under the law, etc. It is almost a "start again" proposition, and a "Let's see if we can try a social experiment that works for all." Like community development, national development will create backlash because there are many people invested in the status quo regardless of their posturing to the contrary. Am I really willing to take a pay cut so that a homeless man has shelter? Am I willing to support mechanisms that allow the disadvantaged to gain opportunities that they cannot now, and that will result in my number of opportunities decreasing? Do I really believe what my religion teaches me about how I should treat others who are less fortunate when it comes to money, equality and mutual love and respect? It is ironic that there is so much inequality in a country that claims to be Christian for the most part.

Quite frankly, I believe there will be cosmetic changes but I doubt that there will be the major changes required for a much more equitable society. The same applies to Canada. There is an appalling amount of racism hidden just below the surface. I suspect the situation in the United States will result in many talking about what a good idea change is but when it comes to making the sacrifices necessary to implement change the wheels will stop turning. I wish I could say something other than this, but help and love may not be as forthcoming as we think they will be in a predominantly me society.

It is ironic that social beings can be so damn unsociable and individualistic. This will be the downfall of society. This should come as no surprise because the essence of a society is social interaction and the thinking that facilitates this is diametrically opposed to the type of individualistic thinking that has become so prevalent. It is like all the people looting and burning businesses when the focus should be on the police murder of George Floyd. It is obviously more important to many to rip off a television or case of beer than to help the black community make its point in a peaceful way to try to improve the relationship between police and young black men and boys. A very sad state of affairs and a good illustration of the type of selfishness that is so prevalent. Then there are the angry who enjoy being angry for the sake of being angry. Can they be led by an articulate leader and learn to channel their energy toward activities with constructive outcomes that instigate positive change? Can those attempting to discredit the whole peaceful demonstration be dealt with, so that they cannot continue, not only their physical, but social destruction as well? I suspect many are white supremacists who feel that they have been given a thumbs up by the present administration to put their racism into action and what better way than to try to discredit peaceful demonstrations opposing the killing of a black man by the police.

The enormity of the work is overwhelming and will clearly not be undertaken by the Trump administration and the GOP old girls' and boys' network. Full-scale change in the White House, the House and the Senate is needed and the sooner the better!

One thing is clear. Change in the United States will occur. The question is whether it will be good for the country, or if the country will topple over the brink into civil war, genocide or something equally horrible.

Young People Should be Angry!

I think many young people are not all that interested in politics but this does not mean they are unaware of what is happening, and perhaps that is why they have tuned out to a large degree. It is difficult to become interested in something like "democracy" when it is so corrupt you feel totally removed from it and do not see how it impacts your life. It is as though you are here and politics are something that happens over there, when you should feel an integral part of the political process. The question is why a person should invest their time and energy in processes that seem totally removed from their lives, even if in reality they have a considerable bearing on their lives. Instead of prayers and anthems in schools, a daily spiel on democracy may be of far greater use. It is just assumed that we all understand democracy and government and will see that we have a responsibility to vote. This is true even when we see politicians in the USA deliberately trying to exclude some voters because they will likely vote against the party that tries to have them ousted.

I hear people talk about how young people should do their civic duty and get out and vote and many do in spite of the politicians moving further from representing them as time passes. I should qualify this comment because where I live, I am very fortunate to have an excellent Member of the Legislative Assembly and Member of Parliament and neither is on the take. In fact, the government in my province is very good, but when I watch United States politics and those in some other provinces and states it is easy to see why young people would be disgusted by it. Of course, this has all been magnified during the Trump presidency, and in Canada by people like Alberta Premier, Jason Kenney. They go off on tangents and act in ways that may be harmful to the people they are paid to represent in the longer term. They also criticize their predecessors but have done a far worse job. It is called talking a good game but when it comes to delivering, they have failed miserably. LeBron James said something yesterday that was quite profound prior to starting a group called More than a Vote with Skylar Diggins-Smith, Jalen Rose and Trae Young. I am not quoting Mr James but he basically said after the Georgia voting debacle that there was little sense in telling people that voting was the way to instigate change if the voting system is corrupt. Or at least that is how I understood his comment and I thought that he hit the nail right on the head. Not only did he do that but he and the three other black basketball players (Jalen Rose is retired) are going to tackle this issue. It made me feel so good because Mr James is absolutely right and it sent a strong message that discrimination and racism is going to be tackled well outside of police killings of black men. I worked in community development in the Arctic for many years and community development is always multi-faceted because problems and solutions are often related and are systemic. They seldom happen in isolation and that is why you need to have people tackling issues on many fronts. At times it will look chaotic but in the end it all works together because the ultimate goal is the same. I would think that Mr James's comments sent a shiver up the spines of those who may have been thinking that the election "irregularities" will come into play to eliminate many voters and give the election to the candidate of their choice and not the candidate who should have won. So what this group is doing is a huge step because without it the same undermining of democracy will occur and change will be stymied by electoral corruption.

Young people must feel they have a reason to become involved in democracy, whether they just vote or become fully immersed in the process. In order for this to happen, the fundamental changes that I discussed earlier need to occur so that the perverted "democratic system" in the United States can evolve into an actual democracy where people are heard and if are legally entitled to vote can do so without people trying to remove this fundamental democratic right. The average citizen and their concerns must take precedence over the concerns and interests of corporations, lobby groups, special interest groups and other national governments. Without the critical relationship between politician and constituent there is no democracy. If a politician is not representing his constituents, who is he representing? Often this is sadly quite clear because the politician is representing themselves and their corporate and special interest group cronies.

I am not advocating that the interests of corporations and special interest groups be ignored but only that there should be legislation that stops them from buying politicians and their support. Do you think that the United States government would have brought in more gun regulations after all the mass shootings if many of the politicians were not receiving money from the National Rifle Association? Politicians, it seems, will not generally voluntarily reject this type of funding, even though they know full well it compromises them, and could result in them being expected to vote in ways that diametrically oppose the best interests of their constituents. This must stop and it cannot be soon enough.

In the United States many environmental protections have been gutted so that companies can dump waste in water systems, and industry comes before all else. Not very bright after the problems in Ringwood, New Jersey, with Ford dumping over 35,000 tons of toxic paint sludge that continues to threaten the state's drinking water. The United States has pulled out of international agreements to lower carbon emissions. Endangered species have had their protections lifted in some cases. So, what is the message to young adults from the Trump administration and the GOP? It would seem to me to be one that says, "We are old and will die soon and could care less about what subsequent generations are left with, provided we can line our pockets and live today as we wish." Extremely selfish, and you would think people like Moscow Mitch and Trump would care about the generations to come since they have kids. Apparently, it is all about them and the future is of little concern, if their actions are indicative of their feelings.

We should not be surprised that many young people are angry. They live in a so-called democracy and are encouraged to vote, provided the GOP is not trying to eliminate their right to vote because they are members of a visible minority, and yet it is safe to assume that many do not feel their interests are being represented when they do vote. When this happens, democracy is damaged. There is little incentive to vote if politicians are more concerned about representing corporations and lobby groups that have contributed to their campaigns than they are about representing the electorate. This is a major problem when so many politicians are being bought and paid for nowadays and are doing the bidding for corporations, foreign interests and lobby groups. Real change must evolve from the grassroots but these are not the people who are out there buying politicians, greasing palms, providing kickbacks, etc. Money is far too significant in politics today in terms of elections, how politicians vote and whose voice is being heard and acted upon. This is another potential cause for an escalation in nastiness and heading closer to the brink. Those who cannot buy politicians want real change, whereas many who can, are quite happy with things as they are, no matter how anti-democratic and disenfranchising they may be for others.

I remember wondering as a young person whether my vote meant anything or not. I wondered if I should not vote as a way of expressing my displeasure with the government of the day. At that time, I worked for an Unemployment Action Centre that was funded by the Alberta Federation of Labour. I thought that voting may be legitimizing a corrupt system and basically giving it a thumbs up by participating in it. Opting out was a good excuse to do nothing. I did not choose to do this and my best friend and I organized public forums on the Lubicon Lake Indian Band conflict with the provincial government and on the right to work. My best friend, Brent, had many good ideas and we put our left-wing ideas into action in a province with Peter Lougheed as Premier. So rather than opting out, I got more involved and it felt like we were having an impact, although I was not big on the conformity that party politics demands. What seemed ideal would be to look for the best solutions to problems, and where they fit on the political spectrum was irrelevant. Aside from that I was told that if I didn't vote, I had no right to complain and I enjoyed complaining because it was an excellent companion for my alcohol abuse at the time. These were strange times and I suppose Brent and I were idealistic, being young people. I met a Welsh man who was very left wing and was a pipefitter by trade. He was absolutely brilliant but would lock himself in his hotel for weeks at a time, getting drunk. He died from alcoholism during one such binge and it made me think about whether I would be able to adopt views that were a better fit within society. I realized that if I couldn't, and could not change the world to fit to my way of thinking, I might suffer the same fate. The onus was on me to adapt and not on the whole world to change. So I slowly began valuing small incremental changes that we could make that were part of a much larger process of change. I also made sure to vote.

I believe to this day that there are many people that have done everything they can to damage the democratic process. Trump and Moscow Mitch McConnell are two such people. McConnell's contempt for the electorate is well known and when he does something that hurts the poor, he seems to take great pleasure in it. Trump, on a number of occasions, has talked about using excessive force and he thinks his powers as President far exceed what they actually do. Last night a bunch of people who were peacefully demonstrating outside the White House were hit with tear gas and rubber bullets so that they would get out of Trump's way so that he could have a photo-op with a Bible in front of a church. Clearly, the kind of thing you would expect to hear about in some banana republic, but not in the country that used to oversee democratic elections in banana republics.

Anger provides energy and it is critical that young people channel their energy to instigate change instead of in destructive ways. Change occurs one person at a time and as more and more people realize Trump is the problem and not part of the solution, the country will be on the way to a slow recovery. This will be the time when things that are not working can be fixed in ways whereby they work for all. It is an opportunity to increase inclusion and participation. It will be an opportunity to demonstrate that economic systems other than the one we have can work in albeit smaller areas to start. COVID-19 too will change many things. I find for example that I used to go to a coffee shop at 5 a.m. every day to write. The coffee shop closed due to the virus so now I go for 5-10 km walks every day at 4:30 a.m. I would never have done this without the virus and the early walks were started with the intention of avoiding others. I have found I really enjoy this change, so even on a personal level COVID-19 has resulted in a positive change in my life and I am grateful. We will see many positive changes resulting from the virus as well.

I am confident in our young people in North America and do not buy all the negative things that are said about them. I am hardly in a position to criticize them when their generation will be the first in many where their future will be less bright than the preceding generation. I will not presume that I know what is good for them when they face COVID-19, global warming, oceans filled with plastic and other major problems too numerous to mention. Past thinking has brought us to this point so anyone with good creative ideas should be listened too and taken seriously whether the status quo likes it or not.

There is a self-help group that has a slogan that basically says that doing the same things expecting different results is insanity. So, continuing on the same path which will destroy the planet is insanity and those that support maintaining the status quo need to be voted out of office at the first opportunity. The planet, our kids and grandkids are depending on it. If we fail them, they will inherit a world not worth inheriting.

The Destructiveness of Partisan Politics

P olitics in democracies are adversarial by their very nature. There is a party or coalition that forms the government and the other parties comprise the opposition. The idea is that the opposition will ensure that the government is held accountable for its decisions and actions. There are a couple of times I can think of when there is not an adversarial relationship between the parties—when someone dies who is well known by both parties, when individuals are freed up from having to vote along party lines to vote with their consciences on issues like euthanasia and abortion, and when there is a crisis where conflict will slow the supply of necessary goods and services for an emergency. There are other instances but the day-to-day business is subject to the adversarial relationship. This works well when the dialogue is civil and constructive debate ensues, because better decisions are made this way.

One critical element to this system is that politicians realize that they have a responsibility to represent all constituents after an election whether they supported the winning candidate or not. If this does not happen, constituents in a riding where their candidate lost would go for four years or more without any political representation. This is not the way a democracy works although there are often debates about whether a constituency is likely to gain more political goodies if they have a member of the government representing them rather than someone in the opposition.

Democracy should be about putting principles before personalities with the objective being to provide the best possible governance.

There are many dirty tricks that can be played in this system that make it less democratic than it should be. For example, pushing through massive omnibus bills that are hundreds of pages thick and there is no way in the allotted time for the opposition to read them, or properly debate all the bills' content. The other nasty aspects of these bills are that there can be many good things in the bill but a number of bad ones. If the opposition opposes the bill the government can claim that the opposition was in opposition to the positive aspects of the omnibus bill. Quite misleading and dishonest but permitted within the rules. Without reasonable time to debate proposed legislation the democratic system does not work as well as it should.

When the adversarial relationships between political parties in a democracy are put before the desire for good governance, for the benefit of all, there is a major problem and that is precisely what we are seeing with the Trump administration. This is called partisan politics. Since the parties compete against each other for power, partisan politics are to be expected.

The problem with partisan politics when taken to the point of stupidity arises when the party that forms the government blocks good legislation simply because another party put it forward, or when the President attacks Governors because they are members of the Democratic Party, rather than his Republican Party. Another problem is when support to communities and states is provided from the Federal Government to some extent based on whether or not a state has a Republican or Democratic Governor, Senators and Congress members. This is an abuse because the President of the United States is responsible for all United States citizens and partisan politics has no place when dealing with riots and COVID-19. The President either does not grasp this or does not care. He has said that he always wins but there is no winning when imposing his will at the expense of any United States citizen. The United States Republican Senate blocked Obama and continues to block good ideas put forward by Democrats. GOP senators supported Trump when he was impeached by Congress in spite of his clear abuse of power. This is another manifestation of partisan politics. The Republican Party supports Trump no matter what he does and how abusive he becomes.

This means that the Republican Party does not hold Trump accountable and in fact is complicit in all that he does, including attacking the leaders of allies, pulling out of the World Health Organization during a pandemic and presumably ordering that innocent people be tear gassed, hit with rubber bullets and other projectiles, although Attorney-General William Barr was said to have directed this attack on demonstrators exercising their First Amendment rights. Moscow Mitch McConnell apparently supported this attack on the peaceful protesters and like a good little puppet, supported Trump's massive abuse of power as he almost always does. In fact, I was reading that Moscow Mitch's three daughters are completely disgusted with their father's unwavering support of Trump no matter the extent of his abuses. Obviously, these ladies have a good mother who instilled in them a moral compass that is seemingly eluding their father at this point in his career. The same may be said for other Republican Senators like Lindsey Graham who used to oppose the stupidity and immorality of Trump but who now seems to totally support Trump, regardless of what he does. It is difficult to understand how long-term politicians like McConnell and Graham have changed to the degree they have. I imagine that with thirty-some years of service, McConnell would have had a rich legacy that was well respected until he jumped on the Trump bandwagon and began supporting all kinds of abuses. The same is true of Graham and these men need to lose in the 2020 election, along with Trump. Rand Paul and Ted Cruz are a couple of others that seem to have the Trump blinkers on and need to go next election. Partisan politics taken to the extreme as it has been by Trump have created a massive chasm in the country and there are those that question whether the country will ever heal from the damage of this presidency. I have little doubt that a civil war will ensue if Trump is re-elected in 2020.

It is frightening to think that Trump has any say in how, where, when and why US nuclear weapons are to be deployed. After the tear gassing and shootings of peaceful protesters with rubber bullets he would seem to be the last person that should be able to authorize force of any kind without the support of a committee of rational human beings.

Making America Great Again includes over 36 million unemployed, over seven million COVID-19 cases, over 190,000 dead from COVID-19, and the demonstrations/riots across the country due to police killing back men and boys, and specifically George Floyd. I hope Trump is finished Making America Great Again because the country cannot take anymore and needs to heal from this presidency and the abuses of the Republican Party.

The irony in all this is that as politicians jumped on the Trump bandwagon the values associated with the Republican Party were lost. Trump has run up the debt and while he now claims he is all about law and order I wonder for who. Obviously, it is not for the criminals given pardons or his political cronies released from jail due to COVID-19, even though there was no COVID-19 in the jail where one of his cronies was released. Law and order had nothing to do with the peaceful demonstrators being attacked with rubber bullets and tear gas. And to think Melania Trump has the audacity to talk to people about not bullying others. I hope law and order is the order of the day and can only hope that it is applied to all equally, including those in political positions at the highest levels. A good start would be to hold the Attorney General legally accountable for the assault on peaceful demonstrators.

Ruining the Country with Impunity

A s I have watched the protests about the police killing George Floyd, I cannot help but think that there is a broader issue than black men being killed by the police. I am in no way trying to minimize this horrific problem but the broader issue encompasses this abuse and is about inequality before the eyes of the law. Not only are black men treated inequitably but so are those people who are poor, those of other minority groups and those who are not politically connected. Why is it, for example, that the rich often settle with the victims of their crimes by paying them a settlement fee when you and I would go to jail if we committed the same crime? Why is it that members of minorities are disproportionately represented in prisons in Canada and the United States? Does the United States Government not see an obvious problem when jails are privately owned and recidivism increases profits? Does it not see that funding prisons on a per diem basis just invites corruption in the form of kickbacks for convictions and filling prison cells? Black men are not just killed more frequently by police but are also thrown in jail more often, which has an impact on their families and communities.

The demonstrations are about black men being killed by police and do not even cover a small fraction of the judicial abuses directed toward black men and women. I say women because they are incarcerated at twice the rate of white women. Black men are incarcerated at five times the rate of white men which obviously leaves many black women as single parents and therefore less able to provide for their children. There is a massive chain reaction that occurs when racial inequality, like that presently being protested against in the United States, occurs. I suspect the same is true in Canada, the statistics should be of great concern to Canadians because aboriginal people make up five per cent of the population but a third of the prisoners. That is truly staggering and something is obviously wrong!

This reminds me of when I would go to conferences on various social problems and they talked about a problem like addictions or HIV and the solutions to it in isolation of so many factors that contributed to it. The inequality issue has to do with education, justice, health care, housing, poverty, funding, inner city and reserve decay, access to basic services like clean water, safety, nutrition, training, employment, child care and anything else that contributes to the wellbeing of people. Isolating one issue does not tackle the enormity of the problem of inequality but perhaps starting with the killing of black men and boys by the police will lead to broader discussions about the general state of the black community and what four hundred years of racism have meant.

It will require patience and long-term government commitments of funding and on-going reform. I remember being involved with a First Nation and I wrote a proposal for $3 million for a healing program for survivors of residential schools. The government would not commit to really long term projects and funding, and yet when you look at the abuses faced by First Nations and Inuit, it was very clear that it would take generations for healing to occur and for people to learn how to do things like parent when they had been taken from their parents as young children, and so on. It will take years for the black community to heal after four hundred years of abuse. Patience, a long-term commitment, no matter how difficult it gets and clear strategies with affixed actions and timelines for implementation are needed. One thing that must be remembered and this has nothing to do with culture in terms of ethnicity, is that change is not easy sometimes even if it is good. For example, if you take a thirty-year old woman who has been homeless since sixteen and who has only had brief part-time work at fast food joints and give her all the opportunities in the world, it may be difficult for her to take advantage of these opportunities because they are not a normal part of her culture. In the same way you can take a man who is used to wearing a $5,000 Armani suit every day and dress him in rags and put him on the street and he has no idea how "street culture" works. In both cases people are out of their element and are not familiar with group norms so it takes time to adapt to greater problems but also greater success sometimes. Immigration can be like this too, because when refuges come from massive refugee camps, they are not thinking about taking upgrading, English and doing many of the other things we may think they should be excited about doing when they first arrive in Canada. It takes considerable time to adapt. If change does not occur to the degree it should, I fear the initial impromptu discussions between organizers and well-meaning politicians may be pointed to in the future as but one more cause of frustration because dialogue did not result in on-going and sustainable change. There need to be measurable, incremental changes toward goals that all parties identify as desirable. These types of meetings tend to be very useful if the people that attend them can outline concrete things they are willing to do to improve the situation.

I have been to far too many meetings where there was a nice chat that accomplished nothing other than wasting taxpayers' dollars. Interagency meetings die very quickly if there are not tangible results. There should be a master plan and meetings and actions should always be focused on advancing the plan in concrete terms. Community development/national development must span from personal growth and development to family development to community, state and national development. Delineating who is responsible for achieving what is critically important so there is always clarity. There must be mechanisms for measurement and this will promote accountability at all levels.

The United States is headed for the brink but with new, hopefully young vibrant politicians and the will of community leaders to embrace change, there is the possibility that the United States could become that which many hoped it could be. It could become a model for addressing inequality and historical injustices, for rooting out corruption and bringing in progressive legislation that heals divisions and brings people together. The United States has reached a critical juncture in its history and it will either implode, or evolve into something many have only dreamed about. Canada has not had an equivalent wake-up call but there is some very nasty deep-seated racism in Canada. I am embarrassed and feel awful about the racism being directed toward the Asian Canadians in Vancouver and other cities in Canada. It is disgraceful and no one should have to live in fear.

I don't expect the black people in the United States feel supported by the President, given the many incidences where he has supported white supremacists and been supported by them with no objection.

One thing that has really surprised me as I saw the United States rapidly head toward the brink of an implosion under the Trump administration is that they have done so many legally questionable, immoral and unethical things with impunity. Nothing has stopped them because the Senate is controlled by the Republicans and they have basically supported everything Trump has tried to do no matter how self-serving or damaging to the fabric of the country. I thought there were more checks and balances and teeth controlling abuses by all United

States politicians but Trump has gotten away with apparent abuse after abuse with no consequence. Half the time when he makes announcements he later has to backtrack when he finds out others hold the power that he thought he had to force things in the direction he thought they should go. Like when he told the states they would be opening their economies but the power to do this lies with the governors. He said he was going to take social media to task but his legal ability to do this is questionable. He said he would deploy active armed services personnel in the states that would not bring the protests under control but his authority to do this has been debated. In November, it is my hope that the Trumps and Moscow Mitchs of the world will be replaced by people who are anxious to play a role in carrying out Making America Great Again for all. Exciting and scary at the same time. The next four years will be critical as to whether the United States can regain its former stature in the world, and if it can create the type of equitable and inclusive society, we are all hoping it can. I know I am hoping for this to be successful and am also hoping that Canada deals with the racism in this country. It is unacceptable in this day and age. There is no time for hate because there is far too much positive work to be done.

There are people out in large numbers from many cultures in many cities together opposing police brutality toward black men and boys. The younger generation standing united together to fight injustice bodes well for the country. It was blatantly obvious that the demonstrations across the country sent the message that this is not just about blacks opposing police brutality toward black men and boys; it is much bigger than this and anyone with any decency, regardless of their colour knows this is totally unacceptable and must stop now.

Leaders Supporting the First Amendment

It is encouraging to hear police chiefs, mayors and governors speaking about people's right to carry out activities, supported by the First Amendment in the United States. These include freedom of speech, the right to peacefully assemble and the right of people to petition the government to redress grievances. I have found this very impressive amid what, for some in authority, must have been very frustrating and stressful times. While the President was involved in the scene where the innocent protesters were tear-gassed, hit with rubber bullets and hit with flash grenades that violated their First Amendment rights, most other people I saw interviewed on television did not like the violence and looting but acknowledged the right of others to exercise these rights peacefully. It seems odd watching this from afar because there have been so many recent attacks on the Constitution and the turning of a blind eye to a lot of them by the GOP. There are many others who see the Constitution as negotiable or as a hindrance to implementing their less democratic agenda. I also got the impression watching television and listening to leaders from various jurisdictions that there is a tolerance for anger and an expectation that it will be expressed after four hundred years of the on-going abuse of black people. Many also have essentially stated that retaliating to violence with violence does nothing but cause an escalation in it. The police in many instances have been amazing and in others not meeting basic policing standards. I would be angry if I got hit with a bottle or rock and in some cases the police have shown amazing restraint. In others, retaliating immediately with tear gas in large quantities appears to have changed peaceful demonstrations into more violent ones. Violence begets violence. That is why for me it is hard to understand the support for gun ownership in the United States, although the idea is to protect private citizens from the government that does have guns and people that know how to use them. This is a fine idea in principle but on a personal level I do not need a gun to protect myself if you do not own one. Watching United States citizens interviewed has been very interesting and there are an awful lot of very good people who care about each other and want to see justice done. The crowds are a rainbow of cultures. I talked with a black lady today from Toronto and she was telling me about police abuses against the black community there. She said I could not understand the situation for black people because of the colour of my skin and she is right. What George Floyd's death did was show white people just how bad the situation is. I admit to a great deal of ignorance because it is not part of my everyday reality. I do know injustice when I see it regardless of the skin colours involved. I do not need to be black to recognize murder when I see it, or to be appalled when I am told about the frequency with which these types of murders occur. I do not need to be black to recognize that this must be stopped immediately; just as police abuse of Aboriginal people in Canada must stop.

I gained hope when police from many munic-ipalities joined the protesters, or engaged in dialogue with them. It cannot be easy if you are a police person and are tarred with the brush of racism and a penchant for using excessive force when in fact the number of police that are like this are presumably a small minority.

One of the problems we have had in Canada is having the police investigate themselves. This also happens in the United States where Internal Affairs divisions within police departments investigate alleged police abuses. After these investigations the public often feels that discipline should be forthcoming but many times there is none. Whether the public is right in these instances or not, the optics are terrible and justice has to be seen to be served. On the one hand, the police have the training and investigative skills to look into allegations of abuse and misconduct, but on the other, it is like having a wolf investigating a bunch of wolves to find out who the bad wolf was that ate the sheep, having dined at the same table.

One of the things the protests around George Floyd's death has done is to give white people a view into the reality of what it means to be a black male in the United Sates. I was fascinated watching the memorial service for George Floyd. Many issues, across many disciplines, ranging from religion to politics were addressed. There were many excellent points made and I gained a much better sense of the severity of the issue and the reality for black families because this has gone on for four hundred years. I saw a television program where Chinese people in Vancouver were being interviewed and many had been subjected to COVID-19 racism—everything from a women being knocked down to being spat on. I was appalled and I thought Canadians were better than that. We have a lot of work to do in Canada to ensure all citizens feel safe and welcome. The difference between the United States and Canada in these two racist scenarios is that the Premier of my province, who is like the Governor of a state, immediately condemned the racism in the strongest possible terms and so did the Prime Minister of Canada. Governors and Mayors are addressing the racism in the United States but the President has made the situation worse, and even his comments about George Floyd's death being unfortunate cannot be taken seriously, given his racist history. His comment about George Floyd being happy looking down from heaven at the improved economy was absolutely horrible but again Republican politicians remained silent.

I think what I find so important about many state and municipal leaders supporting people in exercising their First Amendment rights is that it signals that many still see the Constitution as the guide to the way America should operate. The Constitution does not need fixing, changing or overriding and it gives me a sense of hope that it can be brought back into play in a major way. It provides a framework for the protection of rights and is like a blueprint for a healthy society. So, the Constitution is like a highway and the United States has had many major accidents it has never addressed. Now it is time to get back on the highway, address social ills and inequity within the solid framework of the Constitution.

The Constitution may save the United States from fascism and so may the 2020 election. Fascism was not brought into Germany overnight. It was brought into play through many incremental changes in the same way the GOP has been making incremental changes and attacking the democratic underpinnings of society. The sooner the GOP is powerless the better. You may think this is a foolish thing to say because when the House and Senate are controlled by different parties in the United States, you would think there would be greater accountability and thought put into legislation. Unfortunately, Moscow Mitch took great pride in blocking legislation when Obama was president and has done the same with bills put forward by the Democrats. This creates a logjam of legislation that goes nowhere because of partisan politics. This hurts the country. Change is needed and progressive thought and legislation is required. As a result, there is no place for people like Moscow Mitch McConnel and Donald Trump in a new progressive United States government that puts the people before self-interest and petty, divisive partisan politics.

Education, Funding and Radical Change

I recently wrote a book about racism and said something to the effect that when a police person approaches your car after stopping you, you do not need to worry about providing a bribe or deal with other corruption. Then the George Floyd death occurred a few weeks after this book was published and I realized two things. The first is that perhaps this is the case because I am white and the second is that if I were black in the United States, having the police approach my car may make me fear being killed. I am very sorry that George Floyd died but wonder if there have ever been a few days when white people have learned so much about what is actually happening with black, brown, Asian and aboriginal people in the United States. I see the impact of Floyd's death has also spilled into Canada where racism is being talked about and demonstrated against. With any luck at all it will be brought out of the closet and meaningful steps will be taken to address the inequality and systemic racism in our society. This will require that cultures collaborate because it is often difficult for the dominant culture to see systemic racism. It is often assumed by the dominant culture that "life is just like that." It may be just like that for the dominant culture, but for people in minority groups who have felt the sting of systemic racism, change is needed in the worst way. Members of minority groups are often uniquely qualified to point systemic racism out. It is important to distinguish between three different forms of racism here. There is the type of racism that has carried on seemingly forever through ignorance among those with the power to change it. This can often be seen in systemic racism. For example, a height requirement of six feet in the police force eliminates most women and Asians from jobs in the police force. This type of systemic racism has been seen for what it is in Canada. Tasers can make size less of a factor in the police force.

There is the malicious sort of racism that the Nazis and white supremacists are known for where they verbally, and at times, physically attack people of colour. Then there is the type of racism where racism exists and ignorance is not the problem, but the will to address it is. An example of this would be seeing

Confederate flags fly in some states and the refusal to remove statues that conjure up painful memories for people. People who are white and who want to address racism against people of colour can usually see malicious racism quite easily if they do their homework and know the symbolism and history of the people and their affiliations who have had statues made of them. They will often need help seeing systemic racism because it can be so subtle and white people can be oblivious to it. My point being that some racism is based on ill will and bigotry and some is based on ignorance. Ignorance is generally more easily addressed. You may argue, and would be correct, if you responded to what I have said by saying all racism is based on ignorance and I agree, but there is a difference between those who with education are open to change and those who are not.

I am not trying to minimize the importance of attitudinal and behaviour change, but government commitment to creating equality can be seen in the levels of funding being provided for minority health care, real justice system reform, funding alternative measures to jail for non-violent offenders of colour, equal funding for education for all, and equally funded social services and public housing programs for all. Put bluntly, talk is cheap. Commitment to equality is demonstrated by governments when budgets are released by various levels of government and the pursuit of racial equality is treated as a financial priority. Anything less than this is lip service.

I remember reading a book about urban development in Montreal. The book pointed out how the politicians of the day sought to complete projects like the Olympic Stadium along with other massive projects. These were highly visible projects that garnered a lot of political support. While this was occurring, infrastructure was being neglected, as were many other things that did not bring major attention to the politicians. The costs for the massive projects were huge and major financial problems were inevitable.

My fear is that like addressing infrastructure issues and public housing in Montreal, it will not be politically "sexy" to create large budget lines to make the necessary series of incremental changes, that, while required to create a more equitable society, are not noteworthy individually enough to create a political splash. That is a problem we have with our political system: doing the right thing via a series of small essentially invisible steps is often not politically expedient. So, it is tempting to opt for the large flashy projects that, while politically expedient, will likely do nothing to promote racial equality. Slogging it out day after day in backrooms can result in some excellent results and positive change but it requires an on-going commitment, huge stamina and the political will to stay the course through many administrations. The way things are unfolding in the United States it appears that the election of GOP governments may stop on-going progress in the process of trying to gain racial equality. This is a sad state of affairs and there are good, non-racist Republican politicians but there are many Republican politicians, from municipal councils to the White House, who do not apparently see anything wrong with racism and have in fact actively promoted it.

When I listened to Atlanta Mayor Keisha Lance Bottom's impassioned speech about the riots, I had two thoughts. The first was that she would make an excellent Vice President and I hope Joe Biden selects her as his running mate so that we are likely to see far more movement toward equality. My second thought was how painful it must be to be a mother of four black children knowing full well that many black boys and men are killed by the police. It made me sad and I thought about my life as a kid being told that if I encountered problems, I should approach a policeman (I don't think there were policewomen at the time) and they would help me. I have no idea whether Mayor

Bottoms tells her children if they need to fear and avoid the police. I think the Mayor's comments made me understand the severity of the situation on a day-to-day basis. I have tried to imagine what it must be like living in fear every day when I am supposedly living in a peaceful democratic country that does not have a war occurring on its soil. I do not really understand how this must feel, it is so far outside my reality as a middle class white but I do not want to see anyone living in fear and pain, and I detest racism.

If equality is to be strived for it must begin with lessons in pre-school. It is ironic that two- and three-year olds happily play with children of many different colours and don't appear to think twice about it. So, what goes wrong? Some adult comes along and tells the little kids that differences are sufficient reason for hate. These little kids are taught this. It does not just occur and if the kids ask questions about why other kids are different colours, parents can explain this in a way that promotes tolerance, love and inclusiveness. Education is critical to address racism in North America. If people see equality as important, space needs to be found in the school curriculum to address this issue. And what a critical issue it is when, whether it be work, the arts, social events, sports or almost anything else we must interact with people of other cultures. I feel this enriches life and should be a source of celebration. There are many exercises that can be done in a good way to teach children how racism feels and these should be included in the curriculum.

One of my pet peeves in Canada is when I see racism and the politics of division being ignored because "the economy is doing well." "Leaders" that sow the seeds of division and hate for personal gain and to garner political support have no place in my world. Racism is more than sufficient reason not to vote for someone, no matter what is happening with the economy and many other things. I will not vote for a racist leader and be complicit in the abuse of other Canadians because the economy is good. We need to have each other's back and not tolerate playing off one group against another for political gain. It is totally unacceptable.

Multi-Culturalism Versus the Melting Pot

Canada has a policy of multi-culturalism and the United States is a melting pot. Multi-culturalism makes more sense to me than the melting pot approach to racial and cultural diversity. The multi-cultural approach, in simplistic terms, is an approach that supports several distinct ethnic groups and their cultural practices. The melting pot approach in the United States is based on everyone basically adopting the same cultural values, so the onus is on immigrants to change into whatever being a United States citizen is. If there is only one mould for this, it is reasonable to expect that everyone who moves to the United States is supposed to become like a middle-class white US citizen. I am not sure how people from Sudan, Turkey and Tibet are supposed to do this without rejecting everything they believe and the very essence of who they are. The melting pot approach is problematic in that two individuals do not fit into one mould, let alone people from hundreds of different cultures with different languages, foods, religions, dress and anything else you can imagine trying to fit into one mould.

A multi-cultural approach may frustrate some people because the onus in Canada is on the general population to adapt to the changing cultural diversity in society. So, for example, a lot of the Christian-based religious rituals that occur in some schools in the US do not happen in Canada in public schools because we respect the fact that there are children with many different religions in classrooms today and do not expect them to change to Christianity, or be exposed to the Lord's Prayer daily any more than we would expect a class to listen to Muslim prayers or Buddhist teachings. It can be challenging adapting to the cultural shifts in society but one well worth undertaking if we want an inclusive society. I think our diversity of cultures makes the country far richer. The different languages, clothing, food, beliefs and thinking provides a tremendous opportunity to grow and develop beyond what we know but it can be difficult for people to come to the realization that within the country there is no "us and them" because we are one people in one nation.

Canadians are a diverse group of people who try to work together to build a society that works for all. For example, before we even discuss the languages of immigrants, Canada has two official languages, French and English; the territory of Nunavut also has the Inuit language in addition to French and English as an official language (Inuktitut and Inuinnaqtun). The Northwest Territories has nine official languages in addition to French and English (Chipewyan, Cree, Gwich'in, Inuinnaqtun, Inuktitut, Inuvialuktun, North Slavey, South Slavey and Tłı̨chǫ). All these aboriginal groups are comprised of Canadians but their ability to exercise some degree of autonomy is important to their personal and collective identities and health. No system is perfect but this seems to work well. I don't expect other Canadians to be like me but I expect that we will treat each other with respect and courtesy. I found it helpful when working in a cross-cultural setting to try to reach agreement on what it was we wished to collectively achieve. Then how we achieved our shared goal mattered little to me and this left great room for different ways to achieve the same goal. It also provided many learning opportunities and greater insight into the culture I was working with. There was no right way or wrong way, just different ways.

On a personal level living with many different cultures in an apartment building can be challenging because it seems we sometimes have different ideas about the use of communal space, acceptable noise levels, permissiveness with children and a host of other things. Reasonable human beings who are willing to seek mutually acceptable solutions through compromise usually have little trouble dealing with these differences but of course there are people who are disrespectful of others in all cultures.

You may wonder what all this has to do with the United States moving closer to the brink of a civil war or some horrible violence if things do not change. What it has to do with it is that you have males of white privilege who want to dictate who is an American worthy of equal treatment and who is not. Surprisingly, the most visibly angry, racist, bitter people tend to be middle-aged and older white wealthy males who have had every advantage in life. They have not been discriminated on the basis of gender, race, economic standing or anything else. And yet, some, like Trump need to constantly tweet out racist garbage, continually attack Obama and point out that George Floyd was likely looking down from Heaven a few days after his death, taking great pleasure in the country's economic numbers improving. Could anything have been any more insulting to the deceased man's family?

A good illustration of this problem and sense of privilege is very clear when you see a table full of grey-haired white males actually believing they should have the authority to debate and make decisions about women's reproductive health without a female present. The appalling arrogance and sense that they have the right to make decisions about the bodies of people who are of a completely different gender speaks to their sense of white male privilege and it will be a good thing to see that end. When I see this type of thing, I think of my mother, sister and daughter and wonder how these men could possibly conclude that they do not need to consider the input of the opposite gender, or show the sense to simply stay out of it and let women decide what is best for women. What a novel concept—letting the people most impacted by something decide what is best for them! It is the same with race and many other things when it comes to white privilege because these rich white people see it as their right to make decisions that impact others without consulting them or soliciting their input. This must change and this small minority must have their power pared back in relation to the size of their group and their ability to influence must no longer be determined by the thickness of their wallets. Enough is enough and it is time for those that need power to take it and start instituting change that works for the majority and not for a select few rich people.

The challenge, when it comes to addressing racism, is to create tolerance of diversity because no matter how people of colour try, they cannot fit the white middle class mould that everyone who comes to the country is expected to adhere to. With China and India bursting at the seams with people we can do this the easy way or the hard way. With less than 370 million people in the United States and Canada combined and 1.4 billion people in China and 1.35 billion in India it is reasonable to expect that there will be a mass migration of people from Asia to North America. The cultural diversity in our countries will continue to change whether people like Trump like it or not, so we need frameworks for race relations that are respectful, celebrate diversity and promote inclusiveness. A good start would be to apply these principals within our borders now so that as immigration continues, we have a solid cultural framework that achieves the ends cited above. It would be so good if Canada's and the United States' aboriginal, black, brown and Asian people could feel they are being respected, are treated equally and that they are not only welcome but are needed and wanted in their countries. What type of person would deny a fellow citizen these basic needs?

Has your Neighbour Become a Threat?

No doubt you have noticed, as I have, some of the changes that have occurred since 9-11. There is security everywhere and people have been led to believe that they need to live in constant fear. It is a strange phenomenon and it made little sense when George W. Bush used the term "war on terrorism" when discussing how the United States would respond to the 9-11 attacks. What was really needed was a series of strategic attacks on specific groups that posed a threat to the United States, not an all-out war. Since that time there have been huge increases in security that have nothing to do with 9-11, or terrorism. Since COVID-19 began I have been walking at about 4:30 a.m. each day and without exception I see at least one or two security guards cruising around, checking facilities like a park station and washrooms. Another checks a tree nursery and the park. Why someone would want to break into the tree nursery is beyond me. There is a security company at my apartment but my neighbours today are no more dangerous than they would have been thirty years ago. What has changed is the systematic instilling of fear in the public and the fact there are eyes and ears everywhere. The employment of huge numbers of security staff creates low paying jobs but they don't produce anything. They often heighten costs that are passed along to consumers for things like using parks and campgrounds, accommodations, buying groceries, wine and beer and staying in hotels. I doubt many stop problems that, had they been allowed to escalate, would have cost as much to address as the cost of paying the security guard. We also now have gated communities where only the residents are welcome and they have security staff too. The cost to the consumer for all this security is huge, although having security staff may lessen a business's insurance costs and does provide employment.

When 9-11 occurred, there was significant economic disparity. The haves and have-nots, if you will. It was obvious to people paying attention that if the trend of the rich getting richer and the poor and middle class becoming poorer continued, there would come a point when conflict would inevitably occur. 9-11 provided the perfect excuse to put security staff everywhere, that could report incidents they observed to the police, who would then ensure that the rich could maintain their lavish lifestyles, as the number of poor constantly grew bigger, poorer and angrier. The middle class is being eliminated and many are becoming working poor. When you think about the security guards I am seeing daily they have nothing whatsoever to do with preventing terrorism, but their presence makes people think there is an imminent threat they are being protected against, but who, or what is this threat? I suppose it could a homeless person, the poor or some of the many hooked on drugs, but we do not really want to do much about these problems, so we hire more security staff instead because it is simple and comparatively cheap. The billionaire needs to be able to make many more billions while homeless numbers skyrocket and we do nothing about it. Our billionaire is safe and secure in their gated community and in order to ensure this, we all pay security costs that are built into our transportation and food costs, accommodation costs, municipal service costs etc. I would like to see how many security staff actually prevent problems from occurring that cost as much as the wages they are paid. It is s ridiculous situation. Paranoia is the order of the day and the poor and middle class have been brainwashed into believing that somehow over the past few years their neighbours have become far more dangerous and that protection from them is required. They need to realize that when believing this they are buying into a scheme to protect those who are often part of the problem as they hoard money for the sake of money. They often do not invest their money in ways that would result in construction that would employ many, or in ways that goods and services are produced by people who were unemployed. No, the money essentially leaves the economy.

When you have massive police forces in big U.S. cities and a huge military, it is interesting that the rich are so paranoid that they feel the need for yet another level of security. If they think things will get bad enough to warrant this, maybe it would be better to discuss a more equitable way to distribute wealth and resources. Perhaps they could create more jobs and invest in ways that benefit the communities they live in. Bill Gates and Melinda Gates are a good example of people who are unbelievably wealthy but who have ploughed millions back into the community via free computers for schools, paying for vaccine research, etc. If people like the Donald Trumps of the world were to follow suit, we may even be happy that some people had a lot of wealth because of the way in which they used it to help others. There are other rich people who do good works, but there are others who have great wealth, but it is never enough and they will even go so far as to defraud charities to accumulate more wealth. This type of greed and contempt for groups that need support for good works will eventually backfire. If nothing else it moves the United States closer to the brink of an all-out conflict.

If you think I am guilty of throwing out a conspiracy theory about all the new security since 9-11, ask yourself why a corner store in a town of 2,000 people that employs one or two local police officers needs a security guard. Is it because they are another set of eyes that can report the public to the authorities, because the authorities have a vested interest in protecting the wealthy as the poor and middle class are decimated?

Big Brother in modern times is government that represents corporations and lobby groups that are controlled by the wealthiest citizens. It all ties nicely together so that we pay every day in real cash for the excesses of those who already have far more than they need. If this makes you angry, you can see how it may annoy many people and move the whole country another step closer to the brink. It is all about security protecting the rich who have a vested interest in maintaining an economic system that is working for fewer and fewer as time passes. We see this in the numbers of homeless going through the roof, severe poverty, unemployment and underemployment and pressure on social and health programs that people like Trump apparently want to slash to the point where they are unrecognizable. People would be less likely to get angry about income disparity if they had health care, food stamps when times are tough, and a social safety net, but the U.S Government gave the wealthy a massive tax break and now wants to severely cut health and social programs that are essential for many.

The United States could have a good economy that supports good health and social programs. It needn't be an either-or proposition. But that is exactly the way people like Moscow Mitch and Trump frame this, and it is people like them with their insatiable greed that will eventually bring the system crashing down when minorities, the poor, homeless and what is left of the middle class decide to collectively do something about it.

Divide and Conquer

Growing up and living in Canada I have had the misfortune of seeing the government use conquer and divide tactics with our First Nations to achieve its ends repeatedly even though it has a fiduciary responsibility to First Nations and Inuit. Clearly, divide and conquer tactics are not consistent with the Federal Government's responsibility to foster trust, act in good faith and work in conjunction with aboriginal groups to ensure their wellbeing. The nasty games the Federal Government, along with provincial governments, have played to the detriment of our aboriginal people would take volumes to cover in detail. The point is that a strategy that the various levels of government may employ is to use conquer and divide tactics in the United States by playing off one group against another or giving conflicting messages from different levels of government. It will be important that black, brown, yellow, red people and white people in support of equality do to not allow this to happen and always present a united front. This takes tremendous discipline when a government offers one group some serious goodies and does not offer other groups the same deal. The group being offered the serious goodies needs to decline the goodies unless of course the other groups in the coalition will receive equivalent goodies. Conquer and divide usurps power because what could be a massive coalition becomes a conflict-ridden mess of splinter groups that seemingly cannot agree on anything. In fairness, if you have people living in dangerous housing projects who are offered a way out, one's first instinct would be to jump at the opportunity and accept whatever deal is required to achieve this. It may be a once in a lifetime opportunity but unless all are on board the acceptance of this deal signals the beginning of the end, and the coalition falling apart, and in doing so allowing the inequitable status quo to prevail.

To work in a successful coalition, it is possible for a group to work on group specific goals while also advancing broader coalition goals. Where they conflict, dialogue is required to determine how the group and the coalitions best interests will be served. There will be times when group goals will need to be put aside for the sake of the coalition. Other times, when a group is making serious inroads it could set a precedent that will be beneficial to many, or all, of the groups in the coalition. It is important early on that groups and issues to be tackled by a coalition are clearly identified and are not deviated from. This is because a large coalition that has the power to change things and to access resources will attract fringe elements and every group under the sun that feels it has an axe to grind. The more these groups are involved the less clear the focus of the group will become and the more likely it is that there will be conflict within the group. The initial steps taken by the coalition are absolutely critical. They are like the blueprint for a house and if it takes time to get it right, so be it. Far better than rushing ahead prematurely and later finding out that the foundation has problems due to a lack of proper planning. The five w's and h need to be answered in major detail. Stakeholders must participate so they share ownership of any plans and actions that develop. All stakeholders would be wise to support one plan to move forward, and stick to it. There should be a group spokesperson so that the media always gets a consistent message. The coalition must have the legal ability to handle funds coming in and mechanisms that ensure accountability. There should also be formal dispute resolution mechanisms for sorting out internal conflicts. There are bound to be people on power trips, dishonest people and people who do more harm than good in a huge coalition of groups. These issues must be addressed because the survival of the coalition must come before all else.

There must be thought to ensure that the organization's spending is consistent with the image it wishes to portray. I saw an example of where this did not happen at a labour conference and it was not good. The labour groups at the conference claimed to represent the working class so I found a debate about whether their executive should continue driving Imperial Lebarons at the expense of the workers appalling, to put it mildly. Optics are critically important. You can see how the message and the actions were incongruent, and this reflected very poorly on the organization. In the same way, it would not be a good idea to have a lunch of champagne, steak and lobster at a meeting about improving life in a tent city. It is just good to be aware that behaviour and actions are powerful means of communicating whether anything is said or not. Another tactic that is good but can be very difficult to achieve is to always take the high road when attacked, and you know that with people like Trump and Moscow Mitch in the government, any organization that proposes to change the status quo will likely be mercilessly attacked. By taking the high road people will see the attacks for what they are and when the high road is taken the leader keeps the group focused on what matters, leads by example and provides a stark positive contrast to those doing the attacking. This will increase the group's credibility while decreasing that of the attacking individuals or groups. There is nothing wrong with sending very clear messages in a respectful manner. I found this to be the case where the Mayor of Atlanta simply said that the President needed to keep his mouth shut. It was clear, true and was not a personal attack. Taking the high road does not mean being a patsy but does have to do with clearly and positively framing messages, while refraining from gutter politics, tactics and language.

This will require a long, sustained, highly organized and moral and ethical approach. Change is never easy but many of the best changes in history have only occurred due to conflict. A code of conduct may be a good idea for those involved in the coalition because the group cannot be irreparably harmed because of the behaviour of one or two. A code of conduct lays out behavioural expectations and potential consequences for breaches of them. This eliminates the need for a debate about what is unacceptable behaviour when something happens. Reference can be made to the code of conduct which all participants on the coalition should have signed to indicate that they have read and understood the Code of Conduct. There is so much groundwork and having been a community developer, I cannot imagine the magnitude and complexity of the work involved. I do know that a diverse coalition like the one here will need people to leave their egos at the door, their agency specific goals elsewhere, and work in ways that foster respect and mutual understanding. It is also important to know a little about the cultures involved and how they normally conduct business. By this I mean that groups often have different values that can be seen in the way they conduct meetings. For example, being white when I went to a meeting I wanted to sit down and get on with the business at hand. If this happened with many First Nations people in the meeting, it could often drag on and on, and could be marred by conflict and inefficiency. If, on the other hand white people and First Nations people meet and there is time at the beginning of the meeting for First Nation' people to find out how the families of other members are and to catch up on other business, we could often fly through the agenda because there was a far greater level of comfort in the room. This obviously is a generalization used only as an example.

Some groups expect a meeting at 4:00 p.m. will start at 4:00 p.m. sharp. For other groups a 4:00 p.m. meeting will likely start between 4:30 and 4:45. These little nuances are important and understanding them can help to avoid frustration and conflict. I do not know how black, Latino, Chinese and aboriginal people in the United States normally conduct meetings so cannot comment on this but I am sure there are many people who do know and who could share this information with those who need to know.

I have said this is an enormous project that has the potential to be completely overwhelming but it is so exciting to think about nation building, and trying to rid society of systemic problems in the process. It is an opportunity to include those who have been disenfranchised to make positive changes to the economic, justice, health and social systems so that they serve all in an equitable way. Then if the country can rid itself of the President and the old boys' network in the Senate it will have four years to implement changes that I believe most residents will like when they see them in action.

Can We Stop the Divisive Language?

Conservative, Liberal, Socialist, right-wing, left-wing and many other words that, while convenient to use in the media, have played a major role in dividing the United States. Language has played a major role in moving the United States closer to the brink.

These names are often used foolishly here and in the United States. The media would have us believe that Democrats are the only party interested in children's issues, women's issues and social and health programs. The conservatives are said to be concerned about law and order, fiscal responsibility, lowering taxes and the economy, to name a few. The reality is that most people have interests in the areas of both. For example, I am "left-wing" but realize that social and health programs need a healthy economy to support them. To try to suggest that women and children's issues are the exclusive domain of the left is silly. Obviously, many women are conservatives, so are we to believe they have no interest in issues having to do with their own gender, and the children they birthed because they are "right-wing"? Yes, silly isn't it?

I have seen the word "socialist used so many times in the United States media it is incredible. It is often used incorrectly and United States politicians who clearly know little about the Canadian health care system are quick to condemn it as that ugly word "socialist." If I was involved with the coalition to change America, I would focus on solutions, and the words the media chooses to apply to them would be irrelevant. I don't care where on the political spectrum the person is from who identifies the solution to stop having black men and boys killed by police. I don't care about their party affiliation. All I care about is that this must stop, and it must stop now!

I don't care if you brand Canadian health care conservative, liberal, socialist or alien as long as it works. American politicians use the socialist label as if it is evil.

There have been on-going attempts to gut Obamacare with nothing to replace it in spite of the President saying he would introduce a better health care system. If we can get away from the labels for a minute, I think most Americans would agree that car insurance is a good idea and so is house insurance. So, if it is a good idea to insure these things, why is it not a good idea to pay into a national insurance health care system that covers the health care costs of every single citizen, rich or poor? Which is of greater value, a house, car or a human being, and why would we readily insure a house and car but not the health of a human?

If I had a heart attack right now, I could call the ambulance and may be billed $80 later for use of the ambulance. Not bad when a taxi to the hospital would be $15 or $20. I would be admitted to the hospital and if the doctor decided I needed a heart transplant that would cost $150,000 I would be given one, if a heart were available. I would then stay a few days in the hospital, be given medication, pain killers and be hooked up to all kinds of machines. I would see nurses regularly and the doctor daily. When I was discharged, I would thank the staff for their excellent care, walk out of the hospital without spending a penny out of pocket and go home. No bills, no losing my house, or developing other medical issues due to worrying about my medical bills. No paying $10 for a Kleenex, or headache medication, and no other add-ons because I don't pay directly for any of the costs to do with my operation. All I have to do is recover from the heart attack because all Canadians pay taxes if they make a certain amount of money and these taxes pay for the health care system and the health care of all Canadians. So, call it socialist or whatever else you wish, but the idea of walking out of a hospital with no bill and no fear of going bankrupt, or losing a home must have some appeal to many United States citizens. We don't even pay a premium for health care in my province and believe me, as I age it is nice to know that I can get health care if I need it without new costs beyond what I pay for my taxes. The objection in the United States outside of all the rhetoric is that a system like this treats everyone equally. Since you don't pay for health care directly a homeless person is just as entitled to health care as a billionaire, and as we know many wealthy people expect special treatment. Also, if you have user-pay for health care you get economic and racial segregation which appeals to many wealthy whites because they do not want people who are not white using the same health clinic. I went in to a public health clinic in the United States with a friend and found it quite informative that all the staff and patients were members of minorities.

Are we to believe that Republicans have a monopoly on caring about fiscal responsibility? This is really a bit of a joke, with Trump running up the deficit like it has never been run up before, but that aside, I have not heard any Democrats stand up in the House or Senate, demanding fiscal irresponsibility. I am being silly but you can see that it is the language and how it is used, along with the thinking that accompanies it, that is divisive. The question is not how a thought should be politically characterized or which party came up with the idea, but rather whether or not it is a good idea and worthy of further attention, partisan politics aside. As they say, a closed mind is a terrible thing. I have seen far too much of this over the past three years in United States politics. Good ideas are thrown out because of the party affiliation of the person who presented the idea and good governance is not possible with this type of childish approach to winning and losing. The losers are ultimately the United States citizenry who simply want good governance and programs and services that meet their needs. The theatrics, backstabbing, petty politics, name-calling, tantrums and childishness achieve nothing because the purpose of the House and Senate is to govern, not to provide second-rate entertainment.

The United Sates deserve good governance and that means working within the Constitution and understanding the limitations of one's power—something

President Trump has shown repeatedly that he does not understand. This is a shame, as are the on-going attempts at distracting the public from COVID-19 and other important issues, because creating distractions requires time that the President could use to do something constructive.

Language can be very divisive. From racist tweets to the media portraying Democratic and Republican thought as being black and white with few, if any, grey areas. It is sad to see the divisions in the United States and these must be addressed because there must be constructive dialogue to bring the country back from the brink.

Training and Education

In North Carolina a barber requires 1,528 hours of training but a police officer only requires 620. The exception to this is in Charlotte-Mecklenburg where a police office requires an additional 278 hours of training. In California, a police officer requires fourteen hours of field training but only 664 hours of academy training, whereas to get a cosmetology license in California requires 1,600 hours of training. In Louisiana you require 360 hours of training to become a police officer and 500 hours of training to gain a license as a manicurist. (See https://www.cnn.com/2016/09/28/us/jobs-training-police-trnd/index.html). Police in the United States usually require grade 12 or its GED equivalent. In Canada police generally receive 820 hours of training. In addition to high school graduation they must also have completed at least one year of post-secondary education. A post-secondary certificate, diploma or degree is desirable.

So, people that are carrying guns, and Taser guns, and who can use lethal force have less training than people who may screw up your hair or nails if they have a bad day. Is it any wonder we see poor judgement with some police? The hours of training also show that the states obviously believe being a police officer is simple and almost anyone is capable of becoming one. This may be true in some states and that would seem to be part of the problem. Not everyone should be toting around a gun, and positions like being a police officer, a member of the military and other authoritarian positions are known to attract psychopaths and other dangerous people who are, in part, attracted to these jobs because of the power, weapons and validation they offer the incumbent. The more educated people are, the less they tend to like an authoritarian approach. I think you can see this when considering who comprises Trump's base.

So, in Louisiana you can have police walking around with guns and Taser guns after having 320 hours of training, whereas a manicurist requires 500 hours of training to carry a set of nail clippers around the businesses they work in. Not difficult to see why there is a police problem and that many officers have issues with racism and the use of excessive force. Racism has been linked to rigidity of thought, low intelligence and overall low mental ability. It is then no surprise that police departments would have many racists given the low academic requirements to become a police officer. Funny how nurses, doctors and others who do not carry weapons that can inflict deadly force require many times the education that a police officer requires. Not only that but the police I have talked to basically say that half to three-quarters of their jobs now are dealing with the homeless, addicted and mentally ill. Obviously, police need training in these areas where diplomacy and compassion are often far more important than being able to resort to physical force. This is, because the police in these instances are dealing with the ill and not necessarily the criminal element. Where I live you cannot practice psychology without a PhD, but police with no training in mental health and addictions, and minimal police training are expected to use good judgement when dealing with the issues of these folks. In fairness to the police they must be given the training they need to succeed. If today's inner-city police officers are expected to be half police officer and half social/mental health worker, their training should reflect this.

I worked in a hospital that was subject to scathing articles about overcrowding, people sleeping on cots in the hall and some other issues. Of course, the media failed to mention the thousands of admissions and patients who had been successfully treated. I think the issue with the police is like that. The vast majority are probably very good and are as disgusted by what happened to George Floyd as we are. I was recently downtown and ran into a woman outside the public library and she was somewhat incoherent, and was having obvious mental problems. I asked her some questions and it became clear she was in need of help. Just as I was about to phone the hospital a police officer arrived on the scene from the Victoria Police Department. He was exceptional and took over. I was so impressed by his compassion and gentle approach. It was exactly what was required. I walked away and then regretted I had not gotten his badge number so I could cite his good work in a letter to the police department. I used to only send critical letters to the government but now I like to show my appreciation for good work. The point being that for every negative case we hear about there are probably hundreds that were dealt with in the right way by the police. Racism is a whole different matter though, and the singling out of any group for poor or special police treatment needs to be addressed.

The focus is on police abuses and racism today but this problem permeates all government departments, large work places, professional sports, the entertainment industry and educational institutions. I must say that the National Basketball Association has tried very hard to create an inclusive brand that sends positive messages about tolerance and understanding. Some of the players have been quite political in a very good way, speaking about racism, equality and other social and health issues like COVID-19. The National Football League basically ousted Colin Kaepernick from the league for taking a knee as a statement against police brutality, and he has not had a job since, even though he is a far better quarterback than many who do have jobs. This, in a league where 70% of the players are black but fewer than 10% of the coaches are. Pretty pathetic!

Education about racism is required for all segments of society. Not only do we see racism against blacks but we can also see the displacement of racism. This occurs when a group being subjected to racism becomes racist toward another identifiable racial group. For example, the whites discriminate against the blacks and the blacks discriminate against the Asian community. This is simply an example and I am not suggesting this is occurring with these specific groups but it does happen and must also be addressed. It is an error to assume that someone who is the victim of racism is not also racist, however they may only expresses their racism in situations where there is less likely to be a consequence for doing so. For example, the angry black person who has just been the recipient of a racist comment from a rich white woman may feel hesitant to respond because of the power she assumes the white woman possesses, so she makes a derogatory comment toward an elderly Latino lady on her way home. Instead of one victim there are now two. We can see displacement in many situations. The abused wife takes her anger and pain out on her kids; the worker is chewed out by the boss and does the same to his partner when he gets home. So education about racism needs to be for all and provided from both the perspective of dishing it out and being the recipient of it.

I think with what occurred in Saskatoon, Canada, with the police, and what has been happening in the United States, we need to ask if the scope and length of training and education required to be a gun-carrying police officer is adequate. Is there sufficient cross-cultural training and are minorities welcome in police departments, or are they discriminated against? If they are, the possibility of hiring more minority police is less likely to occur until racism is addressed within police departments. I have wondered if the fact that smaller people are now allowed in many police forces has led to the increased use of Tasers and guns. This is worth exploring. Most racism has at its core fear and this needs to be addressed. For example, a person is a white supremacist because they are insecure and are looking for someone to blame for their inadequacies. Picking on a different race requires no thought so they may decide they do not like black people and hold black people responsible for their inability to create the sort of life they feel they deserve. Truth be told, they are insecure, unhappy, feel inferior and inadequate but rather than doing anything constructive about it, racism is easy and provides a convenient scapegoat.

Unfunding Police Forces

Unfunding police departments may be viewed as union busting, but what is a city like Minneapolis to do when the police department is seen as a threat to a segment of the population they are paid to serve? Unions are paid to protect members. The police members, if like employees in government unions who require protecting, are those who have had disciplinary action directed toward them by management for what are perceived as violations of policy, ethics, and or procedures. A police union is paid to protect police that have had disciplinary action taken against them and this may vary from the theft of office supplies to being suspended for killing an impaired driver. If there are enough bad apples that need to be fired to protect the public, unfunding the police is one option. Unions are required to protect one member whose behaviour can reflect poorly on all. Unfortunately, many good police may be unfunded to get rid of a very small minority of bad police. Unions and management would be wise to negotiate ways to deal with this problem because municipalities have little choice with highly corrupt police departments, or where there are a number of police that pose a threat to the public. This is but one more example of where an individual's rights are seen as being more important than collective rights (the public's right to be free of police brutality, and good police maintaining employment).

In Britain and Wales, it is said that about one in twenty police officers carries a gun. Perhaps this is in part because Britain and Wales do not dish out guns like they are candy, as appears to happen in the United States. Also, community policing and crime prevention do not require guns. Guns seem a good fit with the concept of militarized police forces. I find the militarized police approach offensive, because of the mentality that can accompany it. Police are paid to protect the citizenry and are not at war with them, or shouldn't be.

Police involved in community policing must be intelligent and be able to figure out how to resolve issues without resorting to force as a first option. Crime prevention requires a similar ability and both require excellent human relations and communication skills. I do not agree with unfunding police forces unless massive corruption dictates that it is the only way to protect the public. I do think that if the police spend 50% of their time dealing with the addicted and people with mental health issues, there should be a decrease in police force funding and a corresponding increase to the budgets of agencies that deal with these problems. It makes sense to let the police do what they are qualified to do—police work, and leave the mental health and addiction issues to those who are trained to deal with them.

One of the problems I have seen is that police budgets have continued to grow, whereas many non-governmental agencies dealing with addictions, homelessness and mental health have not seen comparable increases in funding, if any at all. Even from a practical point of view, when police officers where I live make around $52,000-$75,000 plus benefits, these types of wages would go a long way in agencies that deal with the mental health and addictions.

I think the police need to get refocused on community policing and feel that many would be very good in this role if given the opportunity. If cuts were not made to the police department where I live, and additional resources could be found for mental health and addictions support, the police would be better able to respond to the changing demands of police work.

By that I mean focusing more on computer scams and crime, on organized crime and international sex and child trafficking rings. I think the police are likely frustrated because their scope of work has dramatically increased and it takes many hours to unravel computer and phone scams that originate in Nigeria and India, for example. At the same time the police are tasked with ensuring local safety and responding to local crime. Anyone who has worked with unions in a management capacity is well aware of how hard it can be to fire the worst sort of abusive employees in positions that require that they interact with the public. So, while unions protect a couple of bad apples, the employees of whole departments, agencies and businesses get branded with the same brush. I support making it far easier to get rid of abusive police, social services and health care staff. Funding community safety services, mental health, addictions and homelessness by determining actual need would also make sense. Police departments would be well served to get back into community policing and purchase vehicles and weaponry that reflects this. I believe in giving employees the tools they need to do their jobs properly but I think we need to re-examine the use of things like chokeholds, Tasers and other weapons. I think we need to ask why, for example someone was shot in the chest five times when they had a knife and a shot in the leg would have been equally effective at neutralizing the risk they posed to police, or others who were a sufficient distance away from them. In Canada there should be a full review of policing in aboriginal communities and unsolved cases of murdered aboriginal women by an objective third party. There need to be mechanisms to hold the police accountable and that means, for example, that police do not investigate police abuses and that they are investigated by a third outside neutral party. This only makes sense when one reads about the infamous Starlight Tours involving the Saskatoon Police Department and other abuses. Since the police work for the citizenry, and both should have the same goals, accountability only makes sense.

I am not sure what happened but where I live the police have cars that look like military vehicles, which I can see no need for. The police work for us. I have often wondered why they don't use a bunch of electric cars to do their rounds and have a bigger car on immediate call should transportation of people who have been apprehended be required. In many cases we pay for the ambulance, the fire department and the police department to show up to the same incident when one is required. Crime has changed and much occurs online via scams and fraud. So, the nature of policing has changed and it must be difficult for the police to balance the desires of the City Council to have a safe city with people wanting the police to look into scams originating in Nigeria and India. I have been told not to even bother reporting an assault because it will not be seen as being important enough for the police to deal with. I am 59 and I remember the days when people would report stolen bicycles and occasionally the police would find and return them.

In fairness to the police, when many large mental hospitals were closed across the country, many of the patients who were discharged from them eventually became homeless, and in lieu of the proper supports that were often promised when these facilities were closed, the police were forced to do the best they could to deal with the fallout. The police were not trained for this and their workloads skyrocketed as streets in every major city in North America have people desperately needing housing, addiction treatment and mental health services. This was a failure of governments and not of the police.

Some governments have tried to have police on bicycles and horses on the beat and I would imagine this is a good deterrent. I have also seen paramedics on bikes, and street nurses, who are a very good idea. This is the type of community approach that is required. Anyone who knows anything about forensic psychiatry and diseases like schizophrenia knows that some people with mental health issues can be very dangerous. This can also be true of people on some drugs like PCP. So, there is a need for a community approach by the police, social services and health agencies but in the case of the police there are also bad people that need to be removed from society to ensure the safety of the community.

I am not in favour of unfunding the police but I think we need to explore different approaches to public safety. We need to finally address the fallout from closing mental hospitals because some people cannot cope, and never could. They certainly should not be homeless, or ghettoized with the addicted or offenders on parole or probation. The situation is getting worse as the problem magnifies. Part of addressing the problem must be to look at overall program funding within various levels of government, and then all the statistics related to community need, and then to develop new Municipal, Provincial, State and Federal budgets accordingly.

The police and the military have specific roles and both should be to support the citizenry by ensuring their safety against different threats. These needs can vary from helping to stack sandbags to stop a river that is overflowing into a community, to missions to deal with terrorism abroad. The bottom line is that militarized policing seems to take the approach that the citizens that they are paid to protect are the problem. I can see where this comes from and it is classical in-group/out-group stuff. People in the in-group see each other as being different but everyone in the out-group as being the same. This can result in stereotyping, racism, contempt and many other unfavourable approaches by the police toward a community.

When I think about militarized policing and the citizenry being treated like a problem, I am reminded of a day a long time ago when the lights came on for me. I was talking with a man who was complaining about all the money being spent on northern housing for aboriginal people. It dawned on me that this was not about what aboriginal people were getting, or did not get. It was about fellow Canadians needing to meet their basic needs and why would I object to that? Once the race, gender, religious affiliation and sexual orientations of people are taken out of these sorts of discussions, they become about what they should be about: the needs of people who we share the country with. I need to think about whether I would like to save another 10 cents on my next tax return or whether it is more important that a northern community gains clean water to drink.

I think that COVID-19 and the protests in the United States, Canada and elsewhere in the world will result in major positive change. It has not been pleasant and it is very sad that George Floyd was killed, along with so many other black men and boys. I do not think their deaths will have been in vain because they have led us to a place where real change can happen. The type of change that will bode well for the future. One that rejects some benefiting at the expense of others to the same degree, inequitable access to health care, that sees corporate welfare as being more important than food stamps and one that treats the environment as if it is somewhere where future generations will not have to live.

Tackling inequality in its many forms, addressing global warming and stopping countries that desire to take over the world via violence, or economic espionage will be important. Countries that wish to play bully and scoff at the rule of law need to be addressed via groups of allies and the idea that countries like the U.S will go it alone need to give way to practicality and common sense. In many ways we need to get back to what it was like before Trump, with nuclear and environmental agreements, and working toward shared goals as allies. It is not too late, and with the positive momentum, all that is needed is new leadership in the United States in 2020. The world will be a much better place if that happens.

What would make sense is for all those involved serving vulnerable populations and those tasked with providing safety services to meet with open minds to discuss the frustrations, deficiencies, successes, statistics, trends and old ways and new ways of doing things based on the evidence and best practices. The militarization of police forces and the loss of community policing needs to be discussed and how 9-11 created an obsession with security in many different forms. Training and educational issues need to be discussed, given changing social needs, the changes in criminal behaviour and the need for efficient services that support each other but do not duplicate each other. There need to be working groups that are tasked with developing a plan for how social service and health agencies, departments and organizations can meet community needs. Politicians at the three different levels of government can meet later to sort out how budgets need to be adjusted to meet the goals outlined in the plan arising from the working groups. Conceptually, this process would be like putting all the money from all the participant groups in a pot and then determining the extent of needs in various areas and then dividing the money among the groups accordingly. It is like starting again but in doing so creating a system and expenditures that can be rationalized.

The problem with police unions protecting bad police and other unions' bad employees in other disciplines will still exist but management must be willing to document abuses and take the appropriate steps to ensure such abuses do not get repeated.

The National Leadership Void

I am worried about a piecemeal approach to justice reforms in the United States. Each city and state can institute reforms but it would seem to be a good thing for the Federal Government to assume some sort of leadership role whereby it can do whatever it can to coordinate and standardize state initiatives. Otherwise, like in many other service and program areas, there will be completely different rules and systems from city to city and state to state. The argument that each city and state is different and therefore must find solutions that work best for them has some validity, but on the big items like judicial reform and equal access to health care the Federal Government has a role to play. It likely won't, because these are issues involving working toward equality for minorities and this President has shown little, if any, interest in doing this, and in fact is known for his racist tweets.

He is also known for twisting issues so that they fit well for his 2020 election campaign, so I expect that if the Federal Government does anything, it will be about something like police reform and law and order because this completely avoids the issue of racism, the inequitable way people are treated, addressing George Floyd by name, and the broader need for health care, economic and political reform. Trump will want what the Federal Government does to fit his narrative about law and order for election purposes. If that is the case, it will be better for the Federal Government to stay out of reforming anything until there is a competent President that can see beyond their own needs.

I understand that the Minneapolis City Council feels a need to move quickly, given that George Floyd was killed in their city and a CNN crew was jailed there. I just wonder if unfunding the police department should be part of a much larger justice system reform initiative. Until the total scope and plan for justice system reforms is known, it may be difficult to determine what types and amounts of budget allocations will be needed. For example, the reforms could include a whole different way of housing non-violent offenders that is cheaper and more effective, and the money saved could then be directed into education and skills training for these folks.

It would make sense that the unfunding of the police department be coordinated with the hiring of qualified workers of other disciplines to replace them. Are there police officers that may be suitable for other roles within the new system, given the right training? Will there be restorative justice programs, and if so, will the people who run these groups need training? Will new initiatives also include the Asian, aboriginal, white and brown communities? Presumably, the less distinction between ethnicity the better, but there are two strains of thought on this. I once told an aboriginal colleague that I found the program name, National Native Alcohol and Drug Abuse Program, insulting. He said he was glad that the term "Native" was used because it protected the funding for programs specifically for aboriginal people. While cultures are different it may be best to include all ethnicities and focus on commonalities like the collective need for safety, respect, programs that meet basic needs, equal access to health care and the need for judicial system reform, including policing. Given the purpose of the police reforms and racism it would be good community building to have concerned citizens of all colours and cultures come together to work together to create safe, inclusive communities.

The disproportionate incarceration of members of minority groups in the United States and of aboriginal people in Canada must be addressed. This issue requires that reform reach far beyond police reform. It would be interesting comparing sentencing for comparable crimes between whites and minority group members in the United States and whites and aboriginal people in Canada, and see how consistent sentencing is. Presumably, the way a judge sees people has a bearing on sentencing. If a judge sees a victim as being worthless as a result of their ethnicity, an offender may receive a minor sentence for a major crime. If a judge thinks that people from some ethnicities are a far greater threat to society than people from other ones, we should expect to see harsher sentences for these people when compared to people from ethnicities a judge does not harbour these biases about.

Federal leadership will have the present protests referred to in terms of law and order and likely police reform only. This will help to control the wide spread reform that is needed that would result in a more equitable distribution of resources for things like access to health care and education. If the reforms are not wide and sweeping, we will be back at this same place in a few years whether police reform occurs or not. I am not of the impression that the White House or Republicans have any interest in changes beyond cosmetic ones and those that are intended to specifically garner votes in 2020.

The President says he is all about law and order, which is ironic when you consider his background and that of many of his associates. Law and order is about keeping the peace within the framework of the Constitution. It is not about "dominance," pepper spraying people and hitting them with rubber bullets as they peacefully exercise their rights under the First Amendment. It is not about referring to vicious attack dogs and using the military against United States citizens, or having people with weapons who cannot be identified break up peaceful demonstrations. Nor is it about releasing people from prison via pardons who should serve their full sentences. Put simply, the President talks about law and order and plans to be "the President of law and order" heading into the 2020 election but he has not demonstrated any understanding of what this means.

I suppose the leaders of Russia, North Korea, Turkey and China are big on law and order in the same way Trump is, but the Constitution is intended to protect US citizens from exactly what Trump would appear to have in mind for the United States. Very scary times and particularly for those who have escaped persecution in other countries only to find themselves in a country with a President that seemingly wants to move the country toward being a police state. It is not very comforting having the United States as the next door neighbour to Canada either. A border does not stop racism, political intolerance, hateful rhetoric or the abuse of minorities. Both countries have these things, but thankfully, Prime Minister Trudeau does not promote hatred and has provided messages about tolerance and understanding when Chinese Canadians were being targeted for abuse due to COVID-19, something they obviously had nothing to do with.

These are sad but very interesting times. If Trump is re-elected in November, 2020 the United States will continue its downward descent and China and Russia will enjoy increasing amounts of power. The country will become more divided and will likely enter into a civil war or a war with one or more other countries. There has never been a more important election in the history of the United States and I hope Trump is ousted. I along with millions hope the United States that was a world leader and tremendous ally will return. If not, I fear for the people of the United States and the free world.

www.ingramcontent.com/pod-product-compliance
Lightning Source LLC
Chambersburg PA
CBHW061259120726
48001CB00001B/386